The New Plant Parent

Develop Your Green Thumb
and Care for Your House-Plant Family

Darryl Cheng
Creator of House Plant Journal

Abrams Image, New York

Contents

Part I
Caring for Plants

A brass pot complements the green tone of the bird's nest fern (Asplenium nidus).

1. The Plant Parenthood Mentality

The first tagline I used for my blog, House Plant Journal, was: "A journal for my house plants." Although it was completely redundant, I wanted to emphasize that I would be documenting my experiences with my house plants—I enjoyed watching them grow and change. Naturally, when I started out, I looked to books and the Internet for guidance. As I read more and more plant-care advice, I found an imbalance, where the appreciation of house plants was assumed to be mostly visual, while their maintenance was looked upon as a chore, focused on identifying and solving problems. Hardly anyone talked about the long-term satisfaction of owning house plants. Instead, there was an accumulation of "tips and tricks" that would lead one to believe that plants are either super-easy to care for, requiring little consideration of environmental conditions, or finicky drama queens that keel over and die if you don't stand there and mist them every five minutes.

Most plant-care advice is given as a set of instructions tied to individual plant species. The advice reads like a baking recipe that advertises guaranteed results. At the same time, a plant's supposed imperfections are highlighted, and blame is assigned for failure to overcome them: overwatering, underwatering, and so forth. The expectation derived from such advice is that a plant should always look the same or even grow to a state of thriving perfection, except when it mysteriously fails to do so. Reading the reassurance of, "This plant is easy to care for," only adds to one's feelings of being a bad plant parent when a few leaves turn yellow and fall off.

OPPOSITE: Older leaves on this Dracaena marginata naturally fall off as new ones emerge at the tip. Every line on this trunk is the scar of an old leaf. Therefore, know your growing conditions, and let nature take its course—older leaves will fall off.

I think a shift in the plant-care mind-set is needed. In documenting my experiences with house plants, I focused on understanding what environmental factors were most important for house-plant enjoyment. I wasn't looking for perfection—I just wanted to know that I was doing everything I could and that the plant was trying its best too. I applied my engineering thinking to the hobby: optimize my care efforts for maximum house-plant satisfaction. My goal in writing this book is to empower you to understand your home's growing conditions, to be observant, and to accept what nature has in store. It's about equipping you with the right knowledge *and* expectations, so you will know that you're doing the best you can, given the conditions in your home. Finally, I want to help you break away from old habits and ways of thinking that hinder you from truly enjoying plant parenthood.

Easy Versus Hard—What Do You Expect?

Plant experts are constantly telling you which plants are foolproof, but what really makes a particular house plant easy or hard to care for? Of course, a lot has to do with how much effort and patience you're willing to put into its care, but what you expect from the plant is just as important.

Some plants demand attention to prevent permanent damage. Take wilting, for example. When their soil dries out completely, some leafy plants, such as the peace lily and the maidenhair fern, become dramatically wilted. With a good soaking, the peace lily will perk up and look just fine, but the maidenhair fern may not recover. A plant that you can easily kill can be reasonably described as hard to care for, and some plants require more vigilance to keep them alive! Fortunately, as you'll see in this book, most of the plants you will grow are more forgiving.

If you don't want to put time and energy into plant care, growing certain kinds of plants will be hard for you. Growing lots of plants, especially large ones, can be overwhelming if you don't enjoy the process of caring for them. If you need to spend an hour moving plants around simply to water them, you might consider them hard to care for. This book will help you contain your plants for ease of watering and schedule their care sensibly.

If you expect every plant to look "beautiful" all the time and never drop a leaf, then every plant will seem hard to care for. Truly, I tell you, this is an impossible expectation to meet, so get used to removing some dead leaves. Older leaves must die off to balance the resources required for new ones. Most plants develop physical imperfections despite all efforts, and every plant will look different once it has adjusted to living in your home. If you know to expect this, you will learn to appreciate your plants' resourcefulness and character.

And, of course, any plant is hard to care for if you don't understand its needs. Can you give it the amount of light it needs to survive or to thrive? Do you know how to assess soil moisture and how to properly water a plant? The rest of this book should help you develop confidence—you'll know what you're doing! When you understand your growing conditions and care methods, many house-plant "problems" fall into the unavoidable and non-life-threatening category: They are your problems, not the plant's problems. But if you can change your expectations and accept what nature has in store, you'll get great enjoyment from your plants for many years.

ABOVE: Snake plants are classified as "easy" because they can maintain their broad leaves for years even while living several feet from a window, which, as you'll learn, corresponds to lower watering frequency.

RIGHT: When a palm frond becomes yellow and you tried everything to stop it, does that make the palm a hard plant to care for? What if you knew to expect some leaf loss?

Understanding the Adjustment Period

Most of the house plants we buy are grown rapidly in conditions that are nearly impossible to reproduce inside our homes. Thus, every plant you bring home faces an adjustment period. The greater the difference in any of the original growing conditions compared to our homes, the more impact the adjustment period will have on the plant. The most influential factor for plant adjustment is light, because it determines the rate and direction of growth, given adequate water and air flow. And it's not as simple as "there's less sun"; it's the fact that your walls and ceiling are opaque to the sky.

During the adjustment period, there's a risk of older leaves yellowing, leaf tips becoming crispy brown, and of a plant's developing leggy or lopsided growth patterns. After some weeks or months, the rate of leaf death will balance the rate of leaf growth—the plant has stabilized, for now. Sometime after that, the plant will likely take on a new shape optimized for its new home. The next adjustment will come when it is time to repot the plant or replenish the soil. You can suffer through the changes your plants undergo, or you can enjoy the process of helping them through the adjustment period, removing dead leaves and pruning them to a pleasing shape.

OPPOSITE: A monstera is a large plant that can be enjoyed for many years if you have the space!

Subjective Life Span

I call the length of time a plant can be enjoyed, as opposed to how long it can survive, the plant's subjective life span. Just like baby plants that are "not ready for sale" because they appear too small and less presentable, a healthily growing plant may develop to the point where it is no longer aesthetically pleasing or convenient to care for. It can also be the case that some plants just don't stay "nice looking" indoors for very long, although they are still technically alive. Like all living things, a plant changes over time. With luck, you've had years of enjoying it, watching it grow, flower, maybe even produce some offshoots. Now it needs your help, and, fortunately, you have options: You can reshape it by pruning, reset it by pruning (you may be able to propagate tips), or reset it by propagation. Once you know how it grows and how it reproduces, you'll be able to find a way to extend its life. Outdoor gardeners are familiar with perennial and annual plants; indoor gardeners should adopt a similar awareness of the different life cycles of their plants for the sake of enjoying the hobby—you're not taking care of a sculpture!

There are some wonderfully long-lived house plants and even some seemingly immortal ones that can be enjoyed for generations. These plants accomplish everlasting life in two different ways: first, by preserving aesthetic qualities throughout their life span (some with pruning, some without), and second, by producing offshoots, which are essentially clones, for your continued enjoyment. We'll meet some of those, but we'll also learn satisfying skills for regenerating plants that lose their pleasing form.

"Overwatering" Overplayed

When I was starting out with house plants, I kept encountering the command "Don't overwater!" This advice on its own seemed to imply that one should err on the side of watering less. But what, exactly, does this mean? Do I just trickle in some water on a frequent basis? Does it mean to never drench the soil? Because the advice is rarely followed up with specific instructions, people tend to be anxious whenever they start pouring water onto soil. They also think that the act of watering a plant is the caretaker's only responsibility. This book will help you understand that the amount of light a plant receives determines its water usage, and show you how soil aeration helps with maintaining soil structure. When the light is right and the roots are happy, the plant is working. When the plant is working, it will use up water correctly.

"Low Light" Versus No Light

The most important lesson you'll learn from this book is how to gauge the intensity of light a plant is receiving. Light, not fertilizer, is a plant's main food—it's what a plant "eats" to produce carbohydrates. Many articles like to use catchy phrases such as "10 best houseplants for low light" or "thrives in low light," but there's always confusion surrounding the definition of low light and even what it means to be thriving. In general, "low light" is brighter than you think—when horticulturalists say a plant can grow in low light, they are referring to a daily high of 50 to 100 foot-candles. Your windowless office's artificial lighting, while it might seem bright to you, may only be putting out 30 foot-candles at your desk. Yes, a plant might technically survive there, but it can hardly thrive! Truthfully, after watching that plant go through a grueling adjustment period where 80 to 90 percent of its foliage dies off, most people would dismiss it as being dead.

Furthermore, a plant growing in low light typically needs much less water than a plant in bright light. Once you've learned how to be an effective plant parent by tailoring your care to a plant's specific needs based on the environment you've provided for it, you will be far less dependent on all that plant-specific advice that gets recycled on the Internet.

Purpose of Plant Parenthood

The natural world balances life and death, beauty and decay, growth and decline. Beyond the visual enjoyment a well-placed plant provides is the deep satisfaction that comes from caring for its needs, watching it grow, *and even mourning its loss*. Once you understand the adjustment period and accept the concept of a subjective life span for house plants, you will be freed from feeling disappointed and discouraged when you find that your plant has changed. I hope that after reading this book you will come to appreciate the special character a house plant develops after years of ownership and care. And as for the plants you lose interest in over the long term—give them away or experiment with propagation. Focus on understanding your environment, do the best you can for your house plants, and let nature take its course. Those are the hallmarks of a "green thumb."

You'll have a far greater plant parenthood experience if you deepen your appreciation for how plants grow as opposed to simply how they look at a given moment.

LEFT: Fertilizer helps a growing plant. It does not make a plant grow—light makes it grow.

2. A Home for Plants

Take a quick scroll through two of the largest curated house-plant feeds on Instagram, @urbanjungleblog and @houseplantclub. You'll be struck by the appeal of thriving plants growing in the spaces where people live. They convey vitality and the feeling that a place is healthy. And I think you can immediately sense the difference between the space of an authentic plant parent and the "let's brighten up this dark corner with a plant" kind of space.

How? Because the way a plant looks is a direct result of the environment that's been provided for it. That's why I sometimes cringe when I walk past a planter full of nice-looking plants sitting in a mall, under the escalators. "They are basically sent there to die a slow death," says my nursery-owner friend. The key to a plant's sense of belonging in a space is to make sure it's getting the right kind of light.

ABOVE: House plants are often relegated to dark corners because someone confused "low light" with no light. Here's a pothos 'Marble Queen' at the start of what will be a miserable existence.

TOP RIGHT: I saved that pothos by giving her a new home. Now she's basking in bright indirect light from an overhead skylight.

RIGHT: Plants tend to look better when they are photographed in the places where they actually grow. They're saying, "We belong here!" The determining factor is light.

LEFT: Monstera is an eternally popular specimen plant.

BELOW: Wood and terracotta always seem to pair well with plants!

House-Plant Succession

The concept of succession typically refers to how different species of plants dominate a natural community—it could be a forest or a meadow—as it matures. We can think of cycles of house-plant ownership in a similar manner, where you work together with Mother Nature in your home.

Stage 1

Your house-plant succession might start with a specimen plant—a plant whose form and foliage can stand alone as a visual point of interest in a room. The container can either be in harmony with the plant or be bland and unnoticeable (because the focus is on the plant). The classic example is a large floor plant with structural foliage, like a *Dracaena fragrans*. A smaller plant, such as a pothos in a 6-inch pot, can still make a striking specimen if placed in an appropriate location. There's pressure on the single specimen to always shine, so it is wise to choose something that keeps its looks great with minimal maintenance. Considerations for light are often in conflict with décor, but after reading this book you'll be able to find the right spot and level of care for a specimen plant.

Stage 2

When you start acquiring more plants, you'll naturally have areas of your home dedicated to displaying them in groups—the #plantshelfie comes to mind, or a bay window filled with plants. If you want to create a convincing display, bright indirect light should touch every plant (as you'll see, this is another way of saying that each plant should have some view of the sky). Using matching containers is a great way to unify a collection, but don't be afraid to get eclectic with some accents. If you go vertical with your arrangements, be mindful of the compromise among décor, growth conditions, and practicality for maintenance.

Stage 3

You've planted a mature jungle, with foliage everywhere you look. At this point, containers are virtually invisible and may be set up solely for watering convenience (for example, you may have troughs holding groups of plants). As the shapes of trees give a forest character, so the shapes of mature house plants impart character to a room. I think many interior designers would consider an indoor jungle "overgrown," but some would find it enchanting. A truly mature growing space exudes vitality, as though the plants are saying, "We've grown happily here for many years!"

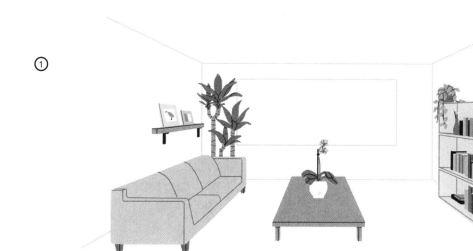

RIGHT: Sometimes, it's more about maturity than abundance. This stairwell has only about a dozen plants; the appeal comes from how they have grown into the space.

BELOW: The mature jungle is more than a room filled with plants; it's really an indoor tropical garden where the plants have grown to suit their environment.

ABOVE AND LEFT: A bay window filled to the brim with plants—accented by a few mature specimen plants.

Styles of House Plants

LEFT: Not my succulents, but I can appreciate when plants are well cared for.

BELOW: My style is tropical foliage—I respond to the diversity of leaf forms, colors, and patterns.

People develop tastes in plants much as they do for different styles of music. I'm partial to tropical foliage, so tropical plants are mostly what you'll find in the journal section of this book. But the sections that discuss plant-care fundamentals can be applied to all plants. Plants all have the same basic needs: the right kind of light, water delivered when needed, and soil management to ensure happy roots. Understanding these concepts will allow you to explore all kinds of plants. By approaching plant care in a holistic manner, you'll develop the knowledge and confidence to observe how any plant responds to your home conditions and give it appropriate care, instead of feeling lost because you were not told the specific instructions for the plant.

3. Understanding House Plants

To care for plants in an understanding way, it helps to know a little bit about how they work. You've probably heard the word *photosynthesis*. Photosynthesis is the way a plant converts the energy in light into chemical energy—that is, into carbohydrates or sugars. When a photon strikes the chlorophyll that gives plant leaves their green color, it powers a reaction between carbon dioxide in the atmosphere and water in the leaf that produces oxygen and carbohydrates. The oxygen is released back into the atmosphere, which is great for animals (like us) that breathe oxygen, and the carbohydrates are used for plant growth. This is the cycle of life for a plant.

Plants, then, are light-eating beings. More than water or fertilizer, a plant's basic food is light. Without the energy from light, a plant starves. In the absence of light that can turn water into life-sustaining carbohydrates, any water that the plant draws up from the soil into its leaves just accumulates in the leaf cells until they burst or drown. And without building blocks of carbohydrates, the plant stops growing. We've all seen a starving plant, off in a corner with no light, its leaves turning brown.

Fortunately, what makes growing plants indoors possible is that different families of plants have different levels of appetite for light. Many tropical foliage plants, in particular, which evolved to live under trees that filter intense sunlight, can thrive without direct sun; they just need some light—the kind we call "bright indirect light"—to be at their best. This is why so many of our most treasured house plants come originally from the tropics. Their light needs are relatively modest, and, coming from a climate where the temperature varies through a narrow range, they can tolerate the temperatures in our homes. But deprive them of enough light, and you're starving them.

OPPOSITE: Neutral-colored pots play nicely with different shades of green.

Commercial growers of tropical foliage plants use shade cloth to weaken the sunlight to just the right amount for rapid growth of their stock, and they use racks that allow water and air to circulate through the pots.

Different Plants for Different Environments

Look at any plant. Its form tells you a lot about its daily needs for light and water. There's a reason there aren't any big leafy dracaenas in the middle of the desert or cute succulents growing on the ground in a rain forest. Thanks to natural selection, plants adapt to make the best use of the light, humidity, temperature, and other conditions in their environment. Leafy tropicals speak to a life lived in an environment where light is attenuated but water is abundant: Their thin, dark green leaves have little room to store water, but they are rich in the chlorophyll required to capture photons that trickle down through a thick canopy of trees. Give them bright indirect light, and your main job will be keeping them consistently moist. Cacti and succulents, on the other hand, evolved to survive desert conditions, where sunlight is intense but water is scarce: Their leaves are pale green moisture fortresses, often guarded by spines. These plants invest less effort in making chlorophyll and more in water storage, so you'll have to make sure that they get loads of sunlight, but in return they'll go a long time between waterings.

As you get to know different families of plants better, you'll become adept at matching specific plants to the growing conditions that you can provide in your home. You'll know which zones in your home provide the bright indirect light that tropicals need. You'll be sparing with water for a plant that isn't getting enough light to metabolize it. And you'll be much less dependent on expert "advice," relying instead on firsthand knowledge and observation.

Adjusting to Home Life Can Be Hard for a Plant

Most of the plants you'll acquire were raised in commercial greenhouses, and, of course, all are descended from plants that evolved in natural settings. Both environments provide a plant with optimal light, water, and soil in ways that you probably won't be able to match in your home. When you remove a plant from an environment that is perfectly in sync with its needs, it will go through a period of adjustment. It's likely to lose some older foliage, and the amount of loss will depend mostly on the decrease in daily ambient light levels that it experiences. I hope that you will come to admire a plant's ability to adjust to a new environment and not despair when it drops some leaves or loses its symmetrical shape. You can save yourself some heartache if you learn to deepen your appreciation for how a plant grows rather than focusing on how it no longer looks as perfect as it did the day you brought it home.

Life in the Nursery

If you think the nursery is a relaxing spa for plants, think again—it is more like an intense training ground. Nursery conditions are optimized for rapid and strong growth to get plants to a sellable size and shape as quickly as possible. Imagine the body of a well-trained athlete—her shape and muscle tone reflect a high standard of training. Now suppose she came to live in your home. Do you have world-class training equipment? Can you provide her the top-notch nutritional supplements she's accustomed to? Probably not—and after a few months of living in your home, her muscle tone will decline. Her shape may even change a bit. Would you say she's dying? Certainly not! Is she still healthy? I'd say she's doing the best she can given her current living situation. It's the same with house plants. If our athlete is losing muscle tone away from the gym, our plants are adjusting to life outside the nursery by letting go of older leaves.

This is what your plants enjoy at a nursery compared to a shop or your home:

Light: A nursery will provide the perfect light intensity for growing most tropical foliage house plants: full sun blocked by a shade cloth. The light will come from directly overhead, unobstructed, to ensure that a plant develops an upright growth structure. Stand next to a window at home and observe how constricted your view of the sky is and how much of it is blocked by the ceiling and walls.

Water: Water at the nursery is probably specially treated to remove chemicals that can cause leaves to get burned. Because no one is worried about getting any floors wet, this treated water can be liberally applied to ensure beautifully even soil moisture. Excess water can easily drain through the pots and onto the ground, where it will eventually evaporate, contributing to the overall humidity. The water you provide to your plant at home is likely to be treated with chlorine and other chemicals—good for you but potentially harmful for your plants. And your watering and drainage surely fall short of factory precision.

Soil management: Most plant nurseries use the same simple planting medium for all their plants, which usually consists of peat and perlite. Nutrients are dissolved directly into the water. Roots are aerated because both the top and bottom of the pots are exposed to air flow (the drainage holes at the bottom of plastic nursery pots also serve to let air in). At home, plants are frequently potted directly into containers with no drainage at all, so soil is often compacted from too little watering or waterlogged from too much.

Air: The air in a nursery is humid and flowing, allowing for efficient gas exchange. Air inside a home is comparatively stale.

Temperature: As a general rule, plants prefer warm days and cool nights. Different plants are optimized to work efficiently at different temperatures, but they all like cooler temperatures when they are resting in the dark. The nursery generally allows a greater difference in day and night temperatures than the average home, which is adjusted for human comfort.

Plant shape: The nursery has the know-how, tools, and conditions to grow a plant into a desirable, and symmetrical, product. When the plant adjusts to life in your home, it will begin to find its own shape as it reaches for the available light.

Life in Nature

If you've ever gone to a tropical forest, where many of our classic house plants originate, you'll find that the plants don't look as "perfect" as they would if they were growing in a nursery. At their best, they look lush and bursting with health, if a bit unkempt. But sometimes, when they're trying to grow a bit outside of their comfort zone, they look to be working to fit in—for example, by reaching up or around an obstacle or producing leaves at the ends of bare stalks. This is an important lesson in plant behavior for the house-plant parent.

This is what your plants enjoy in nature compared with the shop or your home:

Light: "Low light" tropical foliage plants enjoy light filtered through a forest canopy. Even though this is described as "shade," this level of light is still brighter than areas in your home that are far from windows. However, if you keep plants close to windows, you can approximate this kind of light at home.

Water: If house plants could drink from a Holy Grail, it would contain rainwater! And not just any rainwater—the stuff that runs off your roof is far less appealing to plants than rain that drips through a canopy of leaves. You can't provide pure rainwater, but luckily, most tropical house plants can tolerate tap water.

Soil management: Nature is the champion of good soil because of all the critters that make soil their home. Most plants exude sugary substances to attract bacteria, fungi, and their associated food chains. From microbes to insects to animals, these creatures continually replenish soil nutrients and maintain good soil structure that promotes root health. Soil is also kept well aerated as insects and worms burrow near roots. When you bring a plant indoors, you give up all these benefits, but I'll teach you simple techniques to keep soil healthy.

Air: Natural air flow and variance in humidity are familiar to the plant. The air in your home is stale by comparison.

Temperature: Higher daytime temperatures and lower nighttime temperatures are preferred by plants, but our thermostats usually won't allow this. There is much greater variance in nature than in a home or even the nursery.

Plant shape: The rule in nature is survival of the fittest, not survival of the most beautiful! A strong wind or a large animal may bump into a plant, cracking its stem. A hungry herbivore might nibble on a few leaves, only to stop after it dislikes the taste (most tropical foliage plants are a bit poisonous). The point is, a plant growing in the wild will not necessarily conform to a nursery's idea of a salable product. In this sense, it will have more in common with a plant that has adapted to your home environment than with a perfect nursery specimen.

4. Holistic House-Plant Care

A holistic approach to indoor plant care should focus on giving a plant a suitable environment inside your home, observing the plant to assess its needs rather than blindly following directions, and understanding and accepting its life cycle. Most plant-care information is written like the quick, in-passing advice you would get from the plant shop owner just as you're paying for your new plant. It's helpful enough to get you started but rarely enhances your fundamental understanding of plants and long-term expectations of them.

Let's look at the key factors that influence a plant's well-being. Above the soil, there is light, airflow, temperature, and humidity. Below the soil, moisture, airflow, and nutrients. You must decide, as a plant parent, which factors are worth doing something about—to what lengths are you willing to go to ensure the right kind of light? Is it worth your time to raise the humidity around your plants? How much are you willing to adjust your lifestyle to suit your plants?

Factors That Influence House-Plant Health, in Order of Importance

①	Light
②	Water
③	Soil Structure
④	Soil Nutrients
⑤	Temperature
⑥	Humidity

Although all these factors play some role in plant health, the first three—light, watering, and soil structure—are by far the most important. The most helpful general advice I give goes something like this: Make sure your plant receives the right kind of light, that it is watered accordingly, and that its soil is occasionally aerated.

Temperature and humidity are minor factors in plant care for most of the plants you'll be growing because, when dealing with indoor conditions, if we humans are comfortable, most plants will be comfortable. If your indoor temperature and/or humidity is causing you discomfort, you would take action to fix it well before your house plants would complain!

Here are some notes to give you a better picture of the order of importance of the different factors that influence plant health and how they interact.

Light

For any plant, there are three main ranges of light intensity: minimum for survival, good for growth, and maximum for growth. I'm going to give you some tools and techniques to measure light intensity in chapter five. As you'll see when you read some of the plant profiles I've included in this book, the minimum intensity for survival varies by plant, but perhaps more important, some plants look better while starving than others!

Light and watering

The more light a plant receives—measured by both intensity and duration—the more water is consumed in the photosynthesis reaction. And if the plant is in direct sun, it will cool itself by evaporating water through its leaf pores (called stomata). So a growing plant in good light is a thirsty plant. However, if a plant is located in a low-light space, it will metabolize water slowly, and the soil will remain moist longer than it would if it was in bright light. Water that remains in the soil without being used by a plant can cause root rot and other problems. By paying attention to a plant's situation in your home and learning how to gauge how thirsty it is, you can develop a watering strategy that's suited to its needs.

Plant and watering

Succulents have adapted to infrequent rainfall, and they can store water in their leaves to be used during those long dry periods. By contrast, big leafy tropical rain-forest plants rarely need to worry about drought and so they don't store water. In our homes, this plays out by dictating how we are instructed to water a plant: Leafier plants generally prefer evenly moist soil at all times; cacti and succulents like to be completely dry most of the time. With just this much information, and a sensitivity to a plant's light situation, you'll know how much and how often to water most of your plants.

Watering and soil structure:

As a plant repeatedly absorbs moisture, soil particles get pulled together around the roots. Because our containers do not house any insects or worms (we hope), there is no one to loosen the soil to counteract this process, so the soil becomes compacted. You'll learn how to aerate the soil by gently poking it with a chopstick before watering—this loosens the soil and allows air and water to more evenly penetrate.

Light and fertilizer

Fertilizer supplements trace nutrients when they've been depleted from the soil. These nutrients only run out when a plant is growing rapidly. You'll want to fertilize a plant in bright light when you see signs of robust growth. However, if your plant is getting the lower end of the light intensity scale, even if it's growing slowly, you can forgo fertilizer. The trace nutrients in the potting soil itself will probably last until you need to repot, at which time the fresh soil will have a fresh supply of nutrients.

Temperature

The scope of this book is caring for plants indoors, where you live. So long as you are comfortable, the vast majority of house plants will also be comfortable. The most common incidents of plant damage due to temperature occur when they are left in a car. If the outside temperature is such that you wouldn't leave a child in a car, you also shouldn't leave a plant.

Humidity

People hear all kinds tips and tricks about how to raise humidity and how their plants will be sad with the supposed "low humidity of centrally heated homes"—it's borderline fear mongering! If you happen to live in a very dry climate, raising the humidity is best achieved with a humidifier. Don't bother with misting; it's about as effective as trying to heat up a room by lighting a match!

In summary:

· Light is the determining factor in how your plant will grow.

· Other factors should be adjusted based on growth.

· Be realistic in terms of how much you can control these factors.

5. Light

Misunderstanding light intensity is the cause of most disappointing experiences when it comes to house plants. We have vague expressions that describe the amount of light a plant needs in order to thrive: there's sun, partial sun, shade, bright indirect light, and low light. When it comes to house plants, with the exception of cacti and succulents and some flowering plants, most enjoy what horticulturists call "bright indirect light." Plant-care advice tends to leave it at that, quickly moving on to the watering and fertilizing that we, the caretakers, must do for our plants. But what about the job that plants need to do? Their job of growing and living is powered by light! Unless they're getting the right amount of light, all the water and fertilizer in the world will do them no good at all.

I often hear, "My room doesn't get any sunlight." But that room that "doesn't get sunlight" probably has a window, right? How can you tell if your plants are getting the light they need from that window? I've thought about this a great deal, and here's my answer: Only some plants need to see as much sun as possible, but all plants would benefit from seeing as much daytime sky as possible.

Why is light so poorly understood? Think about the environmental conditions that we share with our indoor plants. They generally enjoy the same temperature range that we do, and we're not bad at determining when their soil is moist as opposed to dry, because we can distinguish between degrees of dryness pretty well by touch. Light, on the other hand, is something that animals experience very differently from plants. We humans use light to identify details in our surroundings, whereas plants use it to make their food. So, while we can see effectively into the far corner of a room, away from any windows, a plant living in that corner would be starving—and we would never hear its cries of hunger! In fact, because we need to be able to see what's going on in that corner to survive, evolution has ensured that we have a visual system that isn't good at measuring light intensity—it's optimized to make any scene look as bright as possible, no matter how much light there is. Our eyes can't tell us how much light that plant in the corner is actually getting. So, if light is the prerequisite for proper plant care, we must become better at assessing it. It's time to measure light.

The #WhatMyPlantSees Way of Assessing Light

LEFT: What does this heartleaf philodendron see?

Instead of asking, "How bright is it in this spot?" ask yourself, "What kind of light can my plant see from this spot?" Think about how it changes throughout the day and throughout the seasons. Get your eyes down (or up) to the level of the leaves and *be the plant*! Following a direct line of sight to the nearest window(s), try to identify the following types of light, in order of brightness. You can use this #WhatMyPlant-Sees checklist to develop an awareness of how much light a plant is getting in a specific place in your house.

Type 1, Direct Sun:	The plant has a direct line of sight to the sun. This is the most intense light a plant can receive, and most tropical foliage plants cannot tolerate it for more than three to four hours. Cacti and succulents, on the other hand, prefer it.
Type 2a, Filtered/ Diffused Sun	The plant has a partially obstructed view of the sun. For example, the sun might be shining through trees or through a translucent curtain.
Type 2b, Reflected Sun:	The plant sees shiny objects or surfaces that receive direct sun, even if the plant itself cannot see the sun.
Type 3, Sky Light	The plant sees blue sky on a clear day. This is an easy metric, because while the intensity of the light will change through the day, the amount of sky the plant sees from one position will not.

RIGHT: Viewing from the top shelf, the light seen by the philodendron is entirely type 2b (reflected sun) bouncing through the window and off the white blinds. You can probably tell that the philodendron is getting a relatively low level of bright indirect light compared to plants that are closer to the window, but it's still more than what it would be getting if it couldn't see a window at all. What about the monstera sitting up close to the window—what does it see?

LEFT: The monstera's view is noticeably brighter because of the *larger* view of the blinds (upon which the sun shines— this is type 2b). Also, from this angle, some of the sky can be seen, giving type 3 light—light from the sky.

You'll find that most house plants grow well in *bright indirect light*. A plant in bright indirect light must see any or all of types 2a, 2b, and 3 above. If there are extended times when the plant sees the sun (by getting type 1 light), then you should make sure the plant can tolerate direct sun. When you're estimating light levels using this checklist, the size of your windows and the distance from the plant to the window matters. You can't make your windows bigger, but you can move your plants. The best place for tropical foliage plants will be as close to the windows as possible, with a sheer white curtain to block and diffuse the direct sun—this results in their having the *biggest* view of the sky.

Measuring Light with a Light Meter

You can learn a lot about the amount of light your different plants are getting by using the #WhatMyPlantSees checklist on page 36. Over time, you'll develop a sensitivity to the duration of light and distance from windows. At some point, however, you may want to measure light intensity to test your instincts, and for that you'll need a light meter that measures foot-candles (defined as the brightness of one candle on an area of one square foot at a distance of one foot away). A light meter can demonstrate how rapidly brightness levels decline when you move a plant slightly farther from a window.

In the past, only serious growers would invest in a light meter (you can buy a good one for less than $50). Now there's also an app for that. Smart-phone light meter apps—which range

ABOVE: Here's a room in a high-rise apartment, where large windows and few obstructions mean ideal light for most foliage plants. The windows on the far wall are facing west and on the right wall are facing north. In the following pages, we'll measure the amount of light on the plants keyed in this photograph.

from being free to costing a few dollars—are not as accurate as dedicated light meters, but they are adequate to show you how light intensity varies from place to place. No one will tell you, "This plant must have exactly 375 foot-candles to grow well," but you can learn a lot when you see light intensity dropping by a factor of ten as you walk from one side of your living room to the other. In the photographs for this chapter, I've alternated a dedicated light meter with a smart phone using an app, so you can see both in action.

Once you start measuring light, you'll begin to feel more connected to your plants, as you get a sense of their most basic desire. You'll know they'd starve when you measure only 30 foot-candles along a dark wall. You'll smile as you know your plant is growing happily with 350 foot-candles near the window.

Here's another checklist for bright indirect light, this time as measured by a light meter instead of using the #WhatMyPlantSees approach. Take your readings around the brightest time of the day, which is usually near midday, and try to balance readings for sunny and cloudy days. Hold the meter so that the sensor is next to one of the plant's leaves, facing the nearest light source.

50–150 foot-candles

This is "low light," as in the commonly used phrase "tolerates low light," but it really verges on "no light." Among the plants you're likely to own, only snake plants, pothos, some philodendrons, and ZZ plants will tolerate this level of light. When you get this reading, look up! For a location to be receiving only 50–150 foot-candles at noon on a clear day, the view is probably of a distant window or close to a window with major obstructions—either way, it is a constricted view of the sky.

200–800 foot-candles

This level of light will yield satisfactory growth for all tropical foliage plants, and the "low-light" plants listed above will do much better in this light range. In this range, your plant can probably see a wide view of the sky or the sun shining on a white curtain, and watering can be done with little worry of root rot. Growth, water usage, and soil nutrient depletion will all be faster for a given plant at 400–800 foot-candles as opposed to 200–400 foot-candles. More light than this isn't always better: Keeping your plants in the lower range of light intensity could make them more manageable, as they won't need watering as frequently. You'll sacrifice some growth, but the goal shouldn't be growth just for the sake of it.

800–1,000 foot-candles

A sunny window blocked by a sheer curtain will yield 800 to more than 1,000 foot-candles, and this is the high end of what is acceptable for bright indirect light.

8,000+ foot-candles

Having a direct line of sight with the sun means *very* intense light. Only cacti and succulents enjoy this light level all day. A large tropical foliage plant could tolerate it for several hours, but smaller ones would prefer to be shielded with a sheer curtain.

③ Clear Day

④ Clear Day

③ Cloudy Day

④ Cloudy Day

---

①

Aglaonema is a typical "bright indirect light" plant. At the far side of the room, it still has a good view of the sky because of the floor-to-ceiling windows. On this clear day, I got a reading of 465 foot-candles—this is good light for the Aglaonema.

②

These plants atop the wire shelf are growing happily with 508 foot-candles right now.

---

③ (clear)

The dracaena and jade plants bask in good light: 701 foot-candles. There is no direct sun on any of these plants at this time, but their view is a larger portion of the sky, including some areas *near* the sun.

④ (clear)

A largely unobstructed view of the north sky yields 600 foot-candles.

---

③ (cloudy) and ④ (cloudy)

What happens on a cloudy day? Let's look at locations 3 and 4 on an overcast spring day in the afternoon . . . Because it's an overcast day, the sun's light is diffused evenly but also weakened. Compare the difference in light intensity between locations 3 and 4 on the clear day versus the cloudy day: There's about a 200 foot-candle difference on a clear day; about a 20 foot-candle difference on a cloudy day.

The Low-Light Misunderstanding

This pothos 'Marble Queen' is happily living under a skylight, currently getting 200 foot-candles (top left). Look at #WhatMyPlantSees (bottom left)—at this distance from the skylight, the angle of view of the patch of sky, type 3 light, is rather small, but it is quite bright because the sun is nearby, although not shining directly on the plant.

If we move to a spot where there is a direct line of sight with the sun, the light meter measures above 9,000 foot-candles (top right). #WhatMyPlantSees (bottom right)—the same patch of sky (type 3) from the previous photo, but now we also see the sun (type 1).

If plants had eyes, they would roll them every time someone said the phrase, "thrives in low light." This is simply a justification for using plants purely for décor. I prefer to say of the plant that it "starves gracefully at 50 foot-candles." Specifically, this means the plant will remain relatively good-looking even though it is hanging on for dear life. When horticulturalists use the expression "low light," they are referring to the area under a forest canopy, which is not completely opaque to the sky. The corner of your room farthest from a window is *not* the same—it's more like being inside a cave, looking at a small opening to the outdoors. But don't just take my word for it—measure it!

#WHATMYPLANTSEES VERSUS LIGHT METER READINGS			
Traditional Term	#WhatMyPlantSees (direct and indirect, duration)	Light Meter Readings (foot-candles, duration)	House-Plant Categories
Full Sun	Sees the sun for as many hours of the day as possible (Type 1)	8,000+, as many hours of the day as possible	Cacti will do well; tropical foliage will burn
Partial Sun	Sees the sun for 4–6 hours (Type 1); indirect light (Types 2a, 2b, and 3) for the rest of the day	8,000+ from the sun; 800+ at other times of the day	Succulents and cacti will survive; some tropical foliage will tolerate this sun duration
Shade	Sees the sun for 0–4 hours (Type 1); indirect light (Types 2a, 2b, and 3) for the rest of the day	800+ as many hours of the day as possible	For rapid growth of most foliage plants; succulents and cacti will survive
Bright Indirect Light	Sees the sun for 0–4 hours; indirect light (Types 2a, 2b, and 3) for the rest of the day	400–800 as many hours of the day as possible	For rapid growth of most foliage plants; succulents and cacti may survive
Low Light	Never sees the sun; indirect light all day	200–400 as many hours of the day as possible	For good growth of most foliage plants; not ideal for cacti/succulents
(No light)	Never sees the sun; far from a window	Never brighter than 50–100 for just a few hours	"Low light" plants may survive; cacti/succulents will not grow

Comparing Natural Light with Grow Lights

Now that we're comfortable with measuring light, we can accurately assess the difference in brightness between natural light and grow lights. I'm frequently asked, should I get a grow light to help my plants when I don't have enough sun? After you've measured the light intensity from various lighting situations, you'll realize that no grow light can ever replace the intensity of *direct* sun. If we changed the question to, "when I don't have enough *light*," then we can compare using foot-candle measurements. A grow light provides a helpful reminder that the brightness of light your plant sees is highly dependent on the distance to the source. Turn on your grow light and measure the brightness at different distances from the bulb to the plant.

Notice how quickly the intensity decreases the farther away you go. Take note of these values and compare them with readings you've taken from your windows. A grow light needs to be quite close to your plant for the light intensity to be comparable to that from a big window, even on a cloudy day.

BELOW: Here's a grow light I've set to 12 hours on and 12 off (left). Compare the intensity of light at the position of the philodendron 'Prince of Orange' (center)—564 foot-candles—and, just a few inches away, but farther from the light, at the *Senecio haworthii* (right)—225 foot-candles. How does this compare to natural light?

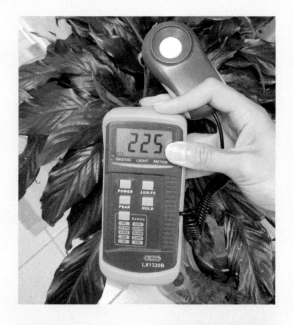

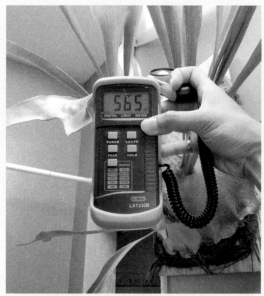

LEFT: My peace lily (top), sitting under the skylight, is getting 225 foot-candles at this moment—equivalent to the *Senecio* haworthii under the grow light. #WhatMyPlantSees (above)—the lily's view of the skylight. No direct sun at the moment, just a view of the sky.

RIGHT: My staghorn fern (top), mounted closer to the skylight, is getting 565 foot-candles (and more if I measured at the very tips of each leaf)—equivalent to the philodendron 'Prince of Orange' under the grow light. #WhatMyPlantSees (above)—the light intensity is greater when the plant is closer to the skylight, because it's seeing more of the sky.

6. Soil

Continuing with the theme of holistic house-plant care, we'll consider soil and watering together as complementary aspects of *soil management*. In the shorter time frame of days to weeks, we need to manage the soil moisture and structure by watering and aeration. For the longer term—several months to years—the depletion of soil nutrients and deterioration of structure should be addressed by repotting, fertilizing, or top dressing. We'll start with soil—its function and components—in this chapter. Then we'll look at the active management of soil moisture, by watering, and structure, by aeration, in the next.

Functions of Soil

There's a lot going on down in the rhizosphere—the area where roots and soil do business. Roots need to anchor into the soil to support the weight of all the plant's aboveground structures (stems, leaves, branches), which requires that soil be of a certain tightness. However, it shouldn't be airtight, as roots also need to exchange gases with the air.

And, of course, soil must hold moisture. This can be tricky. If the soil retains more moisture than the plant can use, roots may die from rot, causing leaves on the plant to yellow and die. Damp, stale soil is also a breeding ground for fungal disease that may infect weakened, rotting roots, causing dark brown spots to appear on leaves. One of these situations will *surely* happen if the plant is starved for light, but if the plant is getting adequate light, one or more of these *may* still happen if stale water accumulates in the soil. On the other hand, if the soil has a high sand content and drains too rapidly, some plants would demand your watering attention on an annoyingly frequent basis just to keep from wilting.

The soil is also where roots find nutrients that support overall plant health. Some elements are dissolved in the moisture found in soils, while others are stuck to soil particles. Without the usual cycling of nutrients found in nature, our house plants must make use of whatever's available in their containers.

Water Retention Versus Drainage

The two main properties of soil that different soil mixes seek to manage are water retention and drainage. These aren't exactly opposites because, as you'll see when we discuss the different components of soil, some mediums can retain water while improving drainage. Water retention refers to the capability of the soil to hold water—think of a sponge absorbing water from a spill. Drainage refers to soil's ability to let excess water fall away as it is poured through. Any medium used for plants will have some capacity for water retention and some drainage characteristics. As we'll see in the next chapter, the way you deliver the water to the soil has an effect on whether it is actually absorbed or whether it drains away.

ABOVE: A close look at a mix of peat moss and perlite—a common potting mix. Peat moss has excellent moisture retention, while perlite imparts drainage and aeration.

Components of House-Plant Soil

Now let's look at some common soil components with respect to water retention and drainage. This is by no means an exhaustive list. There are many other things that can be added to a potting mix, but they all work in basically the same manner: supporting root health and making soil management as convenient as possible. By the way, I'm not saying you must mix your own soil; I simply think you should know how different potting soils are assembled. To put things in perspective, plant nurseries use a mix of peat moss and varying proportions of perlite to grow most of their stock. So if you want to experiment with different mixes, there are many ingredients to try, but if you'd rather not think too much about it, the premade stuff will suffice.

Peat moss
The most widely used main ingredient in potting soil is literally a moss that's harvested from bogs. It acts like a sponge, soaking up lots of water. It has a sweet, earthy smell. Peat moss is rarely used alone as a potting medium.

Coconut coir
A by-product of coconut harvesting, coir is a more sustainable alternative to peat moss. It has spongy properties like peat moss and a slightly sour smell.

Compost (not pictured)
Decayed organic matter, which is widely used for outdoor gardening, is sometimes used for indoor plants as well. It holds water very well and has the added benefit of promoting good soil microbial life. However, the cost of harboring all this life is that it attracts fungus gnats. Compost is typically amended with perlite or coarse sand to improve drainage.

Perlite
The little white rocky bits seen in practically all potting soils is perlite. It is manufactured by heating volcanic glass to a high enough temperature that it pops like popcorn. Thanks to its lower density and larger particle size as compared to peat moss, perlite helps to keep soil fluffy and airy (remember that roots need to exchange gases as well as water). The rough surface of the particle helps hold some water as a film, but not much is absorbed into the particle itself.

Vermiculite
Foamy in structure with a slight golden shimmer, vermiculite is manufactured by heating silicates until they expand into accordion-like particles. Vermiculite is similar to perlite but retains more water.

Coarse sand
Because it has no moisture-absorbing properties, coarse sand is usually added to a potting mix to maintain weight while increasing drainage capability.

Bark chips
Water drains easily through bark chips, thanks to their large particle size, but if they're left soaking for a while—say, thirty minutes—they can hold moisture that will be released slowly. Bark chips are especially useful for good soil structure in larger pots (greater than 12-inch diameter), as the equivalent volume of soil with just peat and perlite would be too dense. Bark chips will eventually decompose.

Sphagnum moss
Having similar properties to a sponge, sphagnum moss retains a lot of water, but when it becomes too dry, it is hard and brittle. You can rehydrate it with a good soaking.

Peat moss

Coconut coir

Perlite

Vermiculite

Coarse sand

Bark chips

Sphagnum moss

RIGHT: My money tree grows well in this peat and perlite mix—roughly two parts peat to one part perlite.

BELOW: Look closely and you'll see grains of sand mixed into this potting mix of small bark chips and peat.

BOTTOM LEFT: My staghorn fern is mounted on a mound of pure sphagnum moss wrapped in burlap. High water retention is needed for mounted plants because there's more surface area exposed to the air, causing more rapid evaporation.

BELOW: My snake plant is potted in a mix of peat, coir, and bark chips. The green beads are slow-release fertilizer granules.

Moisture Capacity of Soil—Weight and Volume

A typical potting mix consisting of peat moss and perlite can absorb about one third its volume of water. If the potting mix contained a greater proportion of coarse sand (as it might if you were growing succulents or cacti), then the total capacity of water that could be absorbed would be reduced to around a quarter or a fifth of the total soil volume. A medium with high water retention, such as sphagnum moss, can absorb up to half its total volume of water. You can rate the mediums described in the section above by their ability to retain water:

· **Highest water retention**
sphagnum moss, peat moss, coir, compost

· **Medium water retention**
vermiculite, bark chips

· **Low water retention**
perlite, coarse sand

Potting soils almost always use a mixture of two or three of these mediums. If you keep perlite or coarse sand on hand, you'll be able to increase the drainage properties of any mix, making it less water retentive.

One way to determine if a plant's soil is dry is simply to lift the pot. The weight will tell you the soil's moisture content: very light = completely dry; heavy = fully saturated. If all other environmental conditions are the same, a plant receiving more light will consume the soil moisture faster (becoming lighter) than a plant sitting in the dark (which will remain heavy). If it's inconvenient to lift the pot, you can use a chopstick to gently probe the soil, as described in the next chapter.

Fertilizer

Plant fertilizers are nutritional supplements providing three main elements:

Nitrogen (N)
Helps with foliage growth.

Phosphorus (P)
Helps with root growth and flower development.

Potassium (K)
Helps with general cellular functions.

Notice how each description says, "helps with" and not "causes" or "makes it grow better." As we saw, plants process carbon dioxide and water into oxygen and carbohydrates. This is a highly simplified description of a very complex system, and additional trace elements are necessary to help plants grow. These are what fertilizer provides.

Any organic matter in the plant's soil already provides some of these nutrients, and the magic trio is also added to commercial potting soil mixes. However, with each watering of a plant, water-soluble nutrients get washed away. If the plant is getting adequate light for good growth and being watered accordingly, it's consuming these trace elements at the same time that they are also being depleted by the watering, and the plant will benefit from having them replenished. However, if your plant is barely growing because you put it where it's only getting daily highs of 50 foot-candles, then you shouldn't bother with fertilizer—simply repotting the plant after a year will replenish the supply of nutrients.

When to Fertilize

When your plant is growing nicely, then you fertilize at the strength and frequency as directed by the manufacturer, or less. Absolutely do not go for more. It's always safer to fertilize less—in fact, one year I experimented with never fertilizing. Of my more established plants, they all lived and grew a few new leaves, but perhaps they could have grown more. Only one plant, a money tree (*Pachira aquatica*), developed leaf discolorations consistent with a magnesium deficiency: Older leaves yellowed while veins remained green. And remember, you're looking for growth. When a plant is just barely scraping by with the minimum light level, it will adjust to this change by dropping older leaves. This is not a sign that you need to fertilize!

You'll note that fertilizer packages are often marked with a sequence of three numbers. These refer to the percentage of nitrogen, phosphorus, and potassium contained in the fertilizer. The ratio will vary across different brands of house-plant fertilizer. Assuming that you're growing house plants for your own pleasure, a "balanced" fertilizer will suffice. I have always used a general-purpose 10-15-10 liquid fertilizer.

7. Water

Routine house-plant care revolves around watering. First-time plant parents struggle with simplistic instructions—"pour some water on the soil once a week" or "don't overwater" are common examples—and often wonder if they're doing the right thing. They may see a plant adjusting to its new home by dropping older leaves, and they'll stress the plant more by watering too much or too little.

In this chapter, we'll try to turn watering from a chore into the positive experience of interacting with a growing plant. In time, you'll learn how much water each plant needs, based on its habits and the amount of light it gets, but first you'll want to make sure that the water you're giving it is reaching the roots. While frequency and amount of watering do play a key role in plant care, there's a bigger picture when it comes to promoting happy roots, and that involves learning some basic watering and soil management practices.

Watering for Even Moisture

The goal of watering your plants is to ensure that soil is moistened correctly. The moisture should be as evenly distributed as possible—this is why soil structure is important. Roots will be happiest when you begin to get a feel for the conditions they're living in, the fluctuating levels of moisture and dryness and the degree of compaction and airiness in the soil around them.

A small amount of water is poured on one spot on the surface of the soil. The water penetrates farthest where the soil is least compacted. Even if it's enough water to find its way to the drainage hole, there may still be some dry pockets of soil. The moisture is unevenly distributed.

In a very dry pot, the soil is often so compacted that it can be seen pulling away from the edges of the pot. No matter how much water you pour in, it will flow along the hardened surface of the soil until it finds the drainage hole, leaving most of the root ball dry. You can wet the roots by submerging the entire pot in a tub of water for an hour, but that's not a realistic watering regimen. There's a more effective and efficient way: soil aeration!

Aerate your soil. Before watering, gently poke a few aeration holes into the soil surface with a chopstick. Now, when water is poured across the surface, it can more evenly penetrate and moisten the soil. It's important to ensure that water is distributed as evenly as possible, since dry pockets of soil can cause roots in those areas to die even when you think you've "watered" the plant.

Three Practical Watering Methods

① Quick Pour

Pour enough water to moisten and penetrate the surface of the soil without causing an overflow at the bottom of the pot. I use this method on a thirsty plant (the kind that prefers evenly moist soil) as a way to hold the plant over until the next time I can do a thorough watering. Take a minute to aerate the soil, especially if the plant is very dry, to facilitate a more even distribution of moisture.

② Continuous Pour Through

This is typically done over the sink. The method involves continually pouring water onto the top of the soil until water runs out through the drainage hole. This method is useful to wash salts that can be harmful out of the soil, but it also leeches away water-soluble nutrients. Every now and then, a plant enjoys a good soaking, and the plant parent can enjoy it too.

③ Pour Through with Soak Up

This is most easily accomplished when the plant is potted in a plastic nursery pot with drainage holes and sits inside a waterproof container or cachepot. You can also move several small plants to a low-walled plastic bin for watering. After a few hours, when the soil has soaked up as much water as possible, you discard the excess. This is a good method for bringing the soil to maximum saturation.

TOP LEFT: Doing the continuous pour through in the shower will allow excess water to drain away.

TOP RIGHT: A good soaking will benefit any plant that is growing nicely in the right light. A pot with drainage holes will allow excess water to drain away, leaving the soil evenly saturated.

BELOW: Smaller plants can be watered in a plastic tub. You can let them sit in water until the soil is saturated, and then put them back in their saucers.

ABOVE: It's important to ensure that water is distributed as evenly as possible, since dry pockets of soil can cause roots in those areas to die even when you think you've "watered" the plant.

Which Method to Use?

All of them! I randomly rotate my watering method and regularly aerate my soil to avoid any imbalances caused by any one of the methods. The quick pour may not reach dry pockets, but it's the least time consuming. The other two methods take more time and space, but you should get accustomed to moving plants around to water them properly. You'll also get used to the needs of different plants: A thirsty maidenhair fern will only stay happy with consistently moist soil, which calls for a thorough soaking every time; a snake plant at a distance from the window will almost always have compacted soil, so you'll be gently loosening the soil each time you water.

Soil Aeration—
The Least Known and Most Helpful Plant Care Technique

When I first started to share my soil-aeration technique, someone commented, "I've successfully grown house plants for years and have never aerated the soil like this!" The truth is, air flows to the roots each time you water—just listen to the crackling as you pour. But as a plant is growing, its roots repeatedly absorb moisture from the surrounding soil, pulling the particles together into dry clumps. If you're really on top of watering moisture-loving plants, the soil structure will never dry out, remaining acceptably loose with each watering. And when you repot the plant, the fresh soil will be nice and airy. The problems of compacted soil arise especially with plants that can tolerate dry soil. Even a good soaking might not moisten the dry clumps, and the plant is at risk of suffocating from lack of airflow. Getting into the habit of soil aeration will help you know each plant's soil better—you can feel its consistency and better judge how compacted it has become.

Remember the illustrations on the nursery, the wild, and the home environments? Both the nursery and the wild have agents of soil aeration, grated work benches and insects respectively. *You* must be the agent of soil aeration for your plants at home. Out in nature, plant roots are accustomed to a dynamic rhizosphere; by comparison, living in a container inside your home will literally bore them to death.

Using a chopstick or any other blunt poker, gently pierce the surface of the soil a short distance away from the main vine (a half inch or more). As you probe, feel the stiffness—with

experience, you will be able to tell if the soil is moist or dry. Wet soil will stick to the probe; lightly moist soil will be soft; dry soil will be brittle and possibly compacted. You are also trying to assess the degree of soil compaction to determine how much you need to loosen it. If you think of the soil as a cylindrical block, the purpose of aeration is to break that block into smaller pieces so that water and air can more easily penetrate. Perlite, vermiculite, and coarse sand can all passively aid in soil aeration, but by aerating the soil with a chopstick, you are effectively taking an active role in managing the soil's structure, just as insects and worms do for plants in the wild.

A good rule of thumb for soil aerating is that plants that require evenly moist soil also enjoy well-aerated soil. Plants that prefer periods of dryness between watering can tolerate more

compacted soils, but since you're watering them less frequently, the likelihood of the soil becoming too compacted is higher. Ideally, you should aerate soils just prior to watering—this way, the action of the water trickling through the soil will help resettle the soil around any roots that are exposed to the air.

Be a bit careful when you poke plants that produce thick, tuberous roots or bulbs. You should avoid piercing these as you aerate, although they regenerate quickly. A short list of such plants: ZZ plant, oxalis, spider plant, asparagus fern, and tuberous begonia (obviously!).

ABOVE: A chopstick makes a good aerator.

Watering Challenges

Your pot has no drainage holes:
If you plant directly into an enclosed container, you need to adjust your watering strategy. First, *do not* put a layer of gravel at the bottom of the container. When water ends up in this layer of gravel, it has nowhere to go. Stale water in a space that gets no fresh air is a recipe for growing bacteria that causes root rot. So skip the drainage layer and ensure that your plant is getting enough light to grow actively and use up soil moisture. As for watering, take care that you do not pour in a volume of water greater than a third of the volume of the soil—think of the soil like a sponge that can only hold so much water; any more and the plant would be swimming in a muddy soup. You can reduce the volume to a quarter or even a fifth of the total soil volume for succulents and cacti. Let the soil soak it all in, and the roots will use up that water before rot has a chance to set in.

Your plant is big and heavy:
You can't put a large plant in the sink, and you don't want water ending up on the floor. The moment you see water draining into the saucer under the plant, stop watering. Keep a turkey baster to draw up the drainage water, as the water can overflow the saucer surprisingly quickly. If there is no drainage hole, then you'll have to estimate the amount of water to add by volume. In either case, it will help to pour the water in slowly to ensure that the soil absorbs as much water as possible. When you pour quickly, the water tends to drain past the soil particles without moistening them.

The Watering Algorithm: Determining *When* to Water

Knowing when to water means knowing the amount of moisture a particular plant likes:

Plant prefers evenly moist soil:

The soil should be kept evenly moist at all times. The moment you see even the surface of the soil become dry, it's time to water. Plants such as maidenhair fern, *Fittonia* (nerve plant), and peace lily enjoy evenly moist soil—mostly these are thin-leaved plants.

Plant prefers partially dry soil:

The soil should be allowed to dry down to an inch or two from the surface. Most foliage house plants are in this category.

Plant prefers completely dry soil:

The soil should be allowed to dry out completely before the next watering. All cacti, succulents, and thick-leaved house plants enjoy completely dry soil, because they store the water needed for photosynthesis in their bodies.

Remember: All watering techniques should be performed on plants that are actively growing. In daily light intensities below 100 foot-candles, even the most resilient "low light" plants will succumb to root rot!

The Pothos Test

You want to water a house plant "whenever the plant needs it." The obvious question then becomes, how do you know when the plant needs it? Try this with a perky pothos (see overleaf): Put the plant in a place where it is getting bright indirect light—say, more than 200 foot-candles at the daytime high. Note how bouncy the foliage is—this is a properly hydrated pothos. Use a chopstick and gently poke around the soil to get a feeling for this evenly moist soil. Now, let the plant grow there, and notice how the leaves will be less bouncy after several days. Feel the soil again with the chopstick—now the soil probably has some dry pockets. This is the point at which you should water, but for the sake of this experiment, don't do it yet. In a day or two more, the leaves will show visible signs of wilting—they are droopy. Now probe the soil with the chopstick: It's probably rocky, stiff, and compacted. What happened over these few days? The soil moisture was continually being absorbed by the roots and transported to the leaves, where some of the water was combined with carbon dioxide to produce sugar. While this happened, the soil particles were being pulled toward the roots. As these soil particles were literally sucked dry, they clumped together into rocky masses. At this point, just pouring some water into the soil won't saturate all the dry pockets that have formed. In the future, for this pothos, you will watch for that first sign of droopiness to know when to water. While this experimental method works well with pothos because of its hardiness, some plants are so sensitive to wilting that they will suffer permanent foliar damage if their soil is left dry for even a day—maidenhair fern, for example. In those cases, instead of observing the plant for signs of dry soil, you should just directly check the soil. On the other hand, many house plants—snake plants and ZZ plants are examples—will not wilt in completely dry soil, and if you really waited until they did, they would be half dead! For these plants, do not aim to keep the soil evenly moist. Give them a thorough watering (and aerating) when the soil becomes bone dry.

LEFT: A 'Marble Queen' pothos going from perky to droopy. The amount of time between these two states varies with many factors—light, temperature, and humidity—so the most reliable approach to watering is to observe the soil and the foliage.

The Well-adjusted Plant

Now that we've looked at both light and water, we can begin to understand how they affect plant growth. The following illustrations will help you understand light, watering, and, most important, plant adjustment.

PLANT A   PLANT B

SITUATION

You bought two identical plants from the nursery and placed them in your home. One plant is closer to the window than the other, but you were instructed to water them once a week. Fortunately for Plant A, the soil became dry enough to need watering again within the week—the moist-to-dry cycle is roughly a week, so the plant stays happy. Notice in the last stage, the oldest leaf has become yellow—this is most likely the result of adjustment to lower light levels compared to the nursery.

Plant B has a different life; being slightly farther away from the window means it is getting much less light. But because you arbitrarily set Sunday as watering day, you continued to water this plant just like Plant A. Look how the soil isn't drying to the same degree in the one-week time frame. When you water it, the soil just becomes more saturated, but that moisture doesn't go into producing carbohydrates for the plant because that requires more light—there is *some* photosynthesis going on, but not much. Instead, water being pumped into the leaves from the roots just sits there until some cells rupture, causing the leaf tips to turn dark brown. If the situation persists, roots can become susceptible to rot, causing the whole plant to eventually die. This is overwatering—prolonged saturated soil *in a low light environment*.

LESSON

Don't blindly follow a schedule for watering. The decision to water should be made by observing the soil and knowing how moist that particular plant prefers its soil.

PLANT A   PLANT B

Now that you've learned how to observe the soil to decide when to water, you adjust the frequency of watering accordingly. Let's say Plant A reaches the appropriate dryness in one week while Plant B, a bit farther from the window, reaches the same dryness in two weeks. Now you're watering according to each plant's moist-to-dry cycle and understanding that the light intensity difference is the reason why the intervals are different

As time passes, you wonder why Plant B seems to have lost more leaves than Plant A. This is the effect of the adjustment period. When you brought those plants home, fresh from the nursery, all that lush foliage was the result of many months (or maybe years) of experiencing ideal conditions for rapid growth. Now, in order to adapt to lower light levels, the plant must let go of older leaves as new ones develop. You wouldn't waste your energy installing a lot of solar panels in a place that doesn't get much sun, right? Many people would deem Plant B to be unhappy, but I see it as simply adjusting to make do with the conditions it has been given. The plant could go on living for many years with just two or three leaves at the top—this is simply how the plant has stabilized to its current conditions. This is why a fresh plant from the nursery always looks out of place if you put it in a windowless corner—it'll have to downsize!

LESSON

Plants will attempt to adjust to whatever conditions they are given, but the results may not always be aesthetically pleasing. Both plants are just doing the best they can given the light they're getting!

PLANT A   PLANT B

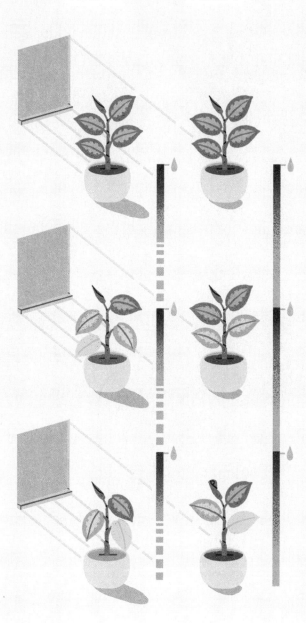

Let's say you're getting lazy and decide to water both plants at the frequency of Plant B, every two weeks. Because Plant A is photosynthesizing faster, its soil will dry out faster. When potting soil becomes very dry, it also becomes compacted and tight. The next time you water, some of the dry pockets may not rehydrate, causing the plant to wilt even after you've watered. If the cycle continues in this way, the compacted soil will not rehydrate until good soil structure has been restored. Letting the soil stay dry for too long also stunts plant growth.

LESSON

Managing the soil means understanding how water flows through the soil as you pour it. Understand that plants receiving a greater intensity of light will require soil remoistening more frequently. Compacted soil should be aerated before watering to facilitate a more even moisture distribution.

Many new plant parents mistake the effects of adjustment to a new home as the plant's dying. A plant needs to let go of older foliage in favor of producing new foliage. Given enough time, the plant will reach an equilibrium point where foliage growth equals foliage loss—the plant is well adjusted— but this doesn't mean it will stay looking the same forever. This is especially true of most tropical foliage plants, as they do not go into a true dormancy period, when all foliage dies back so that new foliage can grow in the next season from tubers or bulbs.

At this point, I hope you can understand why "don't overwater" is not helpful advice. All it does is instill a fear of watering and an intolerance for the circle of life. If you ensure that your plant is getting the right kind of light, water it according to its moisture preferences, and manage its soil structure by occasionally aerating it to prevent soil compaction, it will be happy.

Add a healthy dose of acceptance that nature is about survival and not your aesthetic standards, and you will be on your way to an enjoyable plant parenthood journey.

8. Pruning, Propagation, and Repotting

There are lots of things you can do for your plants under the umbrella of "care." Here I will explain some useful procedures that every plant parent should know how to execute. Consider this proverb I made up:

To keep your plant happy . . .
· for a week: Give it daily light and dark.
· for a month: Maintain proper soil moisture and aerate the soil.
· for several months: Remove dead material.
· for a year: Fertilize and prune it (if applicable).
· for several years: Repot it.

We've covered light and soil management, which includes measuring light, watering, aeration, and fertilizing. Now we'll look at pruning, propagation, and repotting, which are later-stage procedures.

OPPOSITE: Indoor specimens are relatively small compared to how the same species would grow in the wild, so pruning them produces more drastic change than does, say, pruning a tree. However, given time and the right conditions, your plant will continue to grow from the point where you cut it, as in the case of this dracaena. Growers often take advantage of this phenomenon to produce multiply branched specimens of many of the common house plants we know and love.

Pruning

The overall concept of pruning is to cut back certain stems to maintain a desired shape and/or to stimulate branching. Not all house plants need to be pruned, but on some, such as jade plants, stems will bend or break if they are allowed to keep producing leaves without pruning. Often, pruning is about aesthetics—it's a chance for you to decide how you want your plant to look.

Indoor specimens are relatively small compared to how the same species would grow in the wild, so pruning them produces more drastic change than does, say, pruning a tree. However, given time and the right conditions, your plant will continue to grow from the point where you cut it, as in the case of the dracaena on the previous page. Growers often take advantage of this phenomenon to produce multiply branched specimens of many of the common house plants we know and love.

Root Division and Offsets

Root division is essentially dividing a plant at the root level to produce two smaller plants. This works for bushy plants that grow in a compact form, such as ferns, peace lilies, spider plants, and snake plants. With a clean, sharp knife, simply cut the root ball in half and repot the divisions into appropriately sized pots. You should care for the plant as you would any newly repotted plant, providing bright indirect light but not direct sun, and keeping the soil evenly moist. Initially, the two plants will look like halves of plants, but when the roots reestablish themselves, the foliage will fill in nicely.

Occasionally, a plant will put up a miniature version of itself a short distance away from the main stem—snake plants and pilea will do this. When the baby has grown to approximately a third of the size of its mother, you can unpot the plant, cut off the baby with a sharp knife, and repot both mother and baby in separate pots.

Propagation

Propagation is a great way to experiment and learn about how plants develop, but don't expect everything you propagate to grow up looking like the kind of plant you buy from the nursery—unless, of course, you live in a greenhouse! We'll discuss propagation by stem cuttings and leaf cuttings.

ABOVE: Propagation is such a fun part of plant parenthood that dedicated vessels have been designed with elegance in mind.

Stem Cuttings:

Stem cutting is probably the easier of the two methods. You're basically cutting a piece off the main stem of a plant, getting it to grow roots, and transplanting the new plant into soil. This method works best on vines, such as pothos and philodendron. During the rooting, the stem remains submerged in water, which keeps it alive while it's trying to grow new roots.

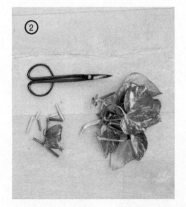

① Pothos 'Golden' and "N'Joy'— ready to take cuttings!

② Cut sections of the main vine so they include a root nub, a stem, and a leaf.

③ You can discard extra pieces of the main vine and any damaged leaves.

④ After a few weeks, you should see some new roots growing from the stem. You can transplant the cuttings into a small pot once the new roots are about an inch long.

⑤ Not only does rooting in water allow you to see when roots develop, you also get to display the cuttings with intriguing glassware—save those interesting bottles or go thrifting for jars and lab glassware!

Leaf Cuttings:

Propagation by leaf cutting is a favorite among succulent owners. Remove a healthy leaf from the plant, place it on a dry surface so it can develop a scab where it was cut (one to two days), then place it onto moist sand (or even put it back into the pot of the main plant). In a few months, a new plant will develop from the base of the old leaf. If you've ever accidentally broken off a succulent leaf and left it sitting on the soil or even on your windowsill, after a few weeks, the leaf will be brimming with young roots and maybe even the tiniest hint of a new plant.

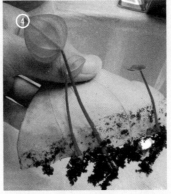

① An army of leaf cuttings from a jade plant rooting in a mixture of peat moss, perlite, and coarse sand.

② Burro's tail (Sedum morgania-num) is a trailing succulent. A few of these burro's tail leaves can be placed onto moist sand and in a few months to a year . . .

③ . . . you'll be able to start the whole process again.

④ A different version of propagation by leaf cutting involves cutting a section of a leaf and inserting the cut edge into the soil. Each vein on the leaf has the potential to root and start a new plant. This method works with peperomia (pictured above), sansevieria, and begonia.

General Tips for Propagators

· Use the sharpest, cleanest knife/pruning shears you can find.

· For stem cuttings, replace the water if you see it getting murky.

· Keep your cuttings away from direct sun; just about any level of indirect light will be fine.

· Keep your cuttings on the warm side. Warmth encourages root growth for typical house plants.

· Be patient. After you transplant your cutting into soil, it will be several weeks or months before you'll have plants that are large enough to enjoy.

Refreshing the Soil (Repotting and Top Dressing)

To repot or not to repot—I know I've had to make this diagnosis many times. Some people overzealously decide to repot immediately after bringing home a new plant from the nursery, thinking that the "cheap plastic pot" just won't do (in fact, those are the best pots for soil management!). Others have the idea floating around in their minds but just never get around to doing it until it is too late, and so their plants suffer to the point of looking terrible—too terrible to be worth the time and effort to care for (remember the subjective life span). While you're deciding (or procrastinating), roots keep getting longer, but in a container, there's nowhere for them to go but out the drainage hole. In a year or so, the roots will have encircled the base of the pot, forming a tight, tangled mass—this is a root-bound plant. These are signs that you need to repot your plant:

· Roots are emerging from the top or bottom of the pot or they are tightly circling the bottom of the pot.

· The soil hasn't been changed for a year or more (depleted nutrients).

· The soil is compacted beyond repair.

· The soil is disintegrated, and particles no longer stick together when wet.

· The plant is not seated at a convenient height.

Aside from seeing physical signs, you should also think about how long the plant has been growing in the same pot. For any of the above situations to occur, the plant would have been growing in its soil for at least a year. So before you diagnose "repotting necessary," look for the signs and consider the length of time the plant has been potted. Finally, anytime you're on the fence about repotting a plant, you can always help it out by giving it a new top dressing. Top dressing is when you remove some of the old soil from the surface of the pot (go down around one to three inches) and add new soil with similar drainage properties to the current soil. Gently mix in the new with the old—it doesn't have to be perfectly mixed; over time, the nutrients in the fresh soil will gradually find their way to the plant's roots.

Pot Sizing: People tend to overestimate the size of pot necessary for their plants, thinking the roots will be "more comfortable" with more space. In general, just a tad cramped is better than too loose. The main reason is this: You want the roots to occupy as much of the soil volume as possible so that, when you moisten the soil, the roots will have access to the moisture. If there are pockets of soil where roots are absent, that area will stay moist longer. Whenever you have a consistently moist and stale environment, there's a chance for root-rot bacteria to breed.

While repotting a root-bound plant, it's important to gently loosen some of the tangled roots. Yes, some of them will break, but they'll grow back stronger. It's best to repot when soil is on the dry side.

Repotting Your Plant

Whenever you take a plant out of its pot, you should take the opportunity to do a few helpful maintenance tasks to ensure that the roots will reestablish themselves as quickly as possible.

1–2.

Unpot the plant: If the pot is planted in a plastic nursery pot, you can squeeze the base of the pot as you gently pull the entire plant out. If the pot is rigid, you can use a small trowel to separate the root ball from the outer edges of the pot as you pull up the plant.

3.

Check for any rotting roots—they'll be dark brown or black and mushy. Remove these!

4.

Gently tease apart the root ball with a chopstick. As much as

possible, avoid breaking roots, but don't worry if you do. It's more important that you untangle the root ball to give the roots a head start in establishing themselves in the new soil.

5.

Cover the drainage hole with a piece of landscape fabric instead of a piece of broken clay pot. Just buy yourself one roll, and it should last you several years of plant parenthood. It's cheap, lets water through, and who has pieces of broken clay pots lying around?

shake the pot to get the soil to settle around the roots—you want the soil to fill in the spaces between the roots.

soil surface, getting soil particles everywhere. Whenever you repot, it's best to get the soil surface to sit a half inch or more below the rim of the pot. This gives the pooled water a chance to trickle down into the rest of the soil.

Fill the bottom of the pot with some soil and tamp it down gently so it is somewhat compressed. The height of this base layer should allow your plant to sit with its soil line about half an inch from the top of the pot. This will make watering more convenient, as you can allow the water to initially pool on the surface of the soil and let it gradually seep down, ensuring an even moisture distribution.

9.

Continue to fill and settle the soil until you reach the top of the pot. Then gently tamp down the soil. It should now sit at least a half inch below the rim of the pot. I'm using a curtain tie to hold up the foliage—makes it easier to see your soil line as you work!

11.

Bring the newly potted plant to the sink or a place where water can drain away, and water the plant thoroughly. Put the plant where it can see as much of the sky as possible but be shielded from the sun. You want the plant to get bright indirect light but not be burned by direct sun. By the next time this plant needs water, you can move it to its usual growing space.

8.
Place the plant in the center of the pot. Using a small trowel/scoop, fill the pot with soil from the sides of the root ball. You can gently

10. If the soil level is even with or above the rim of the pot, proper watering will be an annoying task, since some water will roll off the

9. Pests

When plants are grown at home, they might fall prey to common house-plant pests, because there are no natural predators to control them. Pests are also difficult to notice, especially for the novice grower. Depending on the plant (age, rarity, cost of replacement, and/or sentimental value) and the severity of the infestation, you are entitled to decide that it would be easier to simply discard the plant in the interest of time and for the sake of the rest of your collection. You win some, you lose some!

OPPOSITE: This mealy bug–infested jade plant went through a hard pruning, which will both get rid of many mealy bugs and encourage new growth—a win-win situation!

Prevention

General Methods of Control

Your first line of defense is to avoid bringing infested plants into your home. While at the shop/
nursery, carefully inspect the plant you desire.
Look under the leaves and on the soil surface
for some of the signs described in this chapter. Most reputable nurseries and plant shops
vigilantly inspect their stock daily to eliminate
pests before they take hold. Elsewhere, a freshly
delivered batch of house plants will probably
look fine, but as the weeks go on and the plants
get weaker, they will be more susceptible to
infestation.

Unfortunately, many pests can spawn no
matter how careful we are about what we bring
home. Quite often their eggs are lying dormant,
just waiting for the right conditions for infestation, which usually entails a weak plant. That's
why a healthy plant, growing in the right light
and being watered accordingly, is generally
more resistant to infestation.

House-plant pests spread easily because
of the relatively stable indoor environment and
lack of natural predators. Thus, upon discover-
ing a pest infestation, no matter how small, you
should immediately isolate the plant that hosts
it. When you administer treatments (spraying
foliage or spot-killing), it would be ideal to do it
outdoors or in a large sink, away from your other
plants.

I'm going to give you some general techniques
for pest control. Whichever ones you opt to do,
you should do them with this general approach:
outermost foliage to innermost, top to bottom.
This will minimize the possibility of simply dis-
placing a few pests to another part of the plant
where they can evade your attacks.

Pruning:
Most pests are slow moving and like to congre-
gate at the growing tips of new leaves, so if you
simply prune off those tips, you could be getting
rid of a good portion of the pest population.

Foliar Spray:
Don't expect to completely eradicate the infestation in one go. Pest eggs are extremely resistant to physical assaults, so be prepared to deal
with the pests on regular occasions. It may be
enough to simply keep the pest population under
control at a low level instead of attempting to
completely eradicate them.

Soil Replacement:
For pests that originate from the soil, a good
method of control is to replace as much soil as
possible. It's like a regular repotting except you'll
be removing more soil. It's best to perform this
operation directly into a trash bag.

Common House-Plant Pests (in Order of Increasing Insidiousness)

FUNGUS GNATS

People typically first notice fungus gnats when the adults (small black flies) are seen flying around plants as you disturb them. Their larvae are tiny silvery insects (less than 1 millimeter long) that can be seen crawling around the soil, especially when it's freshly watered. They love moist, compost-rich soil—their name comes from the fact that they feed on fungus.

DAMAGE: Fungus gnats are more of a nuisance than a real danger to your house plants. A few gnats here and there will not harm your plants.

CONTROL: Trap the adults using yellow sticky traps or a bowl of soapy water. If you can find the soil where the larvae are growing, scoop it out and discard the top layer of soil or completely repot the plant. If you're determined, you can avoid using a soil with compost (decaying organic matter). Go with a potting medium labeled "soilless mix," which usually consists of peat moss and perlite. Note that without compost, you will have to supplement the soil nutrition with fertilizer.

ABOVE: A fungus gnat on a money tree.

THRIPS

Adults are a dark brown and crawl away when disturbed. The larvae are translucent yellow and can be found crawling on the surface of leaves.

DAMAGE: Thrips eat away at the surface of the leaf, leaving discolored patches.

CONTROL: Be vigilant in spotting the pale larvae on leaves. If you find them, you can wipe them off with a soapy paper towel. If a leaf is severely infested, it might be safer to just cut it off. Several rounds of spraying the foliage with horticultural oil is also effective if you have the space.

TOP: An adult thrip on a neon pothos—notice the translucent patches. This is leaf damage caused by thrips.
BOTTOM: Thrips larvae are translucent yellow and slightly smaller than the dark adult (center).

MEALY BUGS

The adults have antennae and crawl very slowly when disturbed. Eggs and larvae can be found tucked away in crevices. They appear as white powdery clumps or tiny white specks on leaves.

DAMAGE: Mealy bugs suck the sugar-rich sap out from all parts of the plant but especially new growth. As the bugs multiply and continue to feed, the plant will eventually weaken and die.

CONTROL: Mealy bugs are easy to spot, so the moment you notice anything white and fuzzy on a plant, inspect the plant further. If the infested plant could use a pruning, such as a jade plant, you can start by pruning off most of the infested sections. The remaining bugs can be killed by dabbing them with a cotton swab soaked in rubbing alcohol. Most thicker-leaved plants can withstand the drying effect of the alcohol, but for more delicate foliage, such as a *Fittonia*, you may have to resort to using tweezers to remove the bugs.

ABOVE: Mealy bugs on a jade plant.

SPIDER MITES

For any plants that bask in sunshine in a dry environment, be on the lookout for fine webbing in leaf crevices. If spotted, inspect more closely and you may be able to see tiny yellowish or light brown insects (less than 1 millimeter).

DAMAGE: Spider mites will suck out the precious sap that plants produce. As they attack newly formed buds, those leaves will develop deformities and discolorations. If left unchecked, spider mites can kill an entire plant and spread to others in your collection!

CONTROL: Prune off severely infested leaves/stems. That should cut out a good portion of the population, as the mites enjoy young, tender plant material—consider it forced pruning. Next, buy some horticultural oil, neem oil, or castile soap (not dish detergent). Mix it into a spray bottle—usually a tablespoon per quart of water (try using distilled water if your tap water is particularly hard). The water should be lukewarm. Before spraying, I would cover the surface of the soil with plastic bags so the mites don't just fall back into the soil. Spray down the entire plant with the mixture. Let it sit for an hour or so, then spray off with water. You may have to do the spraying procedure several times. Spider mites are very difficult to completely eradicate, because their eggs are microscopic and hide in all the cracks and crevices along the plant.

OPPOSITE TOP: Spider mites on a Dracaena 'Torch Cane.'
ABOVE: Grainy patches on the undersides of leaves—a classic sign of spider mite damage.

SCALE

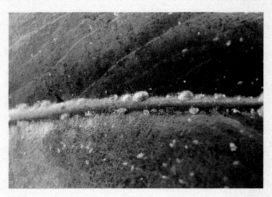

If you see immobile brown or black spots clustered around stems or on leaves, you have a scale infestation. The younger scale insects can crawl very slowly and have visible legs. As they find a suitable location, they stop and develop a protective dome.

DAMAGE: Just like spider mites, scale will suck the sap from plants. Your once-pristine leaves will be covered by brownish bumps. A very severe infestation can kill an entire plant—but you'll probably want to discard the plant well before that.

CONTROL: Pruning is very effective, since scale are mostly immobile. It's also effective to use a cotton swab soaked with rubbing alcohol to do spot-killing. For the remainder of the infestation, you can use the same spray formulation that controls spider mites. Apply this spray on a weekly basis, interspersed with some spot-killing. If this sounds like too much work, consider throwing away the plant—it may not be worth your sanity to try for complete eradication.

ABOVE: Scale insects on a monstera leaf.

10. Acquiring House Plants

Where can I buy that plant? I can never really answer that question. If I have a certain plant, it's because I found it at some store at some point in time. Because there are so many different species and cultivars of plants, a nursery or plant shop will typically rotate its stock. Your local nursery will import baby plants to be potted and grown to sellable size, often depending on what's on offer from larger wholesalers.

This is why I frequent my local nurseries so often—I'm always on the lookout for interesting varieties to add to my collection. It can be helpful to ask the nursery staff whether they can acquire a specific plant—if enough people ask, it may make it worthwhile for the nursery to bring that plant in.

Here's what you can expect when you're shopping for plants in different kinds of stores.

OPPOSITE: Plant nursery shopping spree.

TOP LEFT: Plant nurseries have an amazing selection of house plants.
TOP RIGHT: The plant swap: Trading cuttings at a plant swap is an economical way to get new plants, and it's always fun chatting with other plant parents.
MIDDLE LEFT: It's often difficult to choose that one favorite specimen at a nursery. I'm going to need a few hours to browse these burro's tails.
MIDDLE RIGHT: This leggy dieffenbachia was "free to a good home."
LEFT: Specialty plant shops always have inviting displays.

Nursery: Nurseries usually have the best selection of plants. If you are looking for a great specimen of a particular plant, your best bet is a nursery. The plants you'll find at nurseries are stronger and healthier than plants that have been light-starved for weeks in other retail locations. Nurseries have the best growing conditions and a staff dedicated to plant care!

Specialty plant shop: These are usually staffed by people who love plants and would be very willing to help you choose one or ten. The charm of the little plant shop is that the décor ideas are very accessible, helping you imagine that potted plant in your own space. And there's often a unique selection of planters, sometimes handmade by local artists.

Big-box store: Here you'll find the cheapest prices, and the selection can be surprisingly good. However, the space allocated to plants is usually not illuminated adequately for their growth, which means the stock is slowly dying. (When a plant gets watered in one of these stores, its roots will often begin to rot.) If you get one when it's fresh, you're rescuing it. One exception: a big-box store with a garden center. The garden center is usually open from spring to fall and is a well-lit space where plants can continue growing while they await adoption. If you're looking for a good specimen of a commonly available species, you'll likely find it here at the lowest price.

Grocery store: You're probably getting the same stuff you'd find at big-box stores. The selection is usually quite limited.

Convenience store: It seems to me that many convenience store owners are also plant lovers! As the name implies, the locations are convenient. Although the selection tends to be small, you may find something you've been searching for.

Classified ads: As plants age, some owners lose interest in caring for them—they've reached the end of their subjective life span for that owner. Plants are often put up for adoption, "free to a good home." If you're savvy with pruning and repotting, these acquisitions are a cheap way to build up your collection. As a bonus, you're likely to get unusual-looking specimens, as plants will always take on the character of their surroundings and level of care. But on that note, do beware of bringing home an infested plant—neglected, sickly plants are often prime targets for pests.

Trading/Internet groups: Getting together with like-minded plant parents is a fun way to expand your knowledge and appreciation for how others take care of plants. It's quite easy to find a group of local plant lovers who are willing to trade cuttings and plant stories. Growing plants from cuttings is the ultimate test of patience, but it can be a very rewarding experience.

The plant swap: Trading cuttings at a plant swap is an economical way to get new plants, and it's always fun chatting with other plant parents.

Social media: This one is more for the retailers and suppliers—you can learn a lot about the demand for a particular plant by perusing the feeds of popular house-plant accounts and seeing which images have the highest engagement. As of this writing, popular house plants include fiddle-leaf fig, monstera, and pilea.

Tips for Plant Hunting

LEFT: Coming home.
OPPOSITE: These babies
need more time in the
nursery.

Scout for pests: Wherever you shop, before you start looking for specific plants, do a once-over of the entire space. Any pests are a red flag—you'd be better off leaving before you're tempted to buy an enticing specimen. Bringing home an infested plant is risky, as the pest may spread to fresh hosts.

Buy the size you want now: Remember, the nursery is an intense plant training ground. It has the conditions necessary for producing high-quality specimens. It will be an accomplishment if you can maintain a handsome specimen intact for one year in your home. That's why you should have an idea of the size of plant you wish to own and purchase one at that size. If you're adventurous, you can try buying a smaller one to see how it grows, but don't expect a 4-inch potted dracaena to grow up to look just like the 8-inch potted specimen next to it.

Bringing it home: The key to transporting plants in your car is stabilizing the pot and minimizing foliage damage. If you ask nicely, a nursery will usually have boxes or plant trays you can use.

11. Helpful Tools

As with any hobby, using the right tools makes chores more enjoyable. It's also fun to discover alternate uses for everyday items—or "hacks," as the millennials like to say.

① Watering Can

Now that you understand the kind of control you need to deliver water to your house plants, it's time to invest in a good watering can. Look for a long spout: It's essential to control the direction of the stream and maneuver it in and around the base of the foliage. And make sure that the can you buy fits under your sink faucets! A well-balanced, long-spouted watering can is a beautiful thing. You might even want to have several scattered around your growing spaces!

② Chopstick/Aerator

I find that a chopstick makes an ideal soil aerator because the blunt tip minimizes root damage as you aerate. The stainless-steel kind last longer than wooden, disposable types, which tend to degrade after a few months of watering. I keep several in the soil of various plants—there's always one within arm's reach.

OPPOSITE: Make sure you won't mind looking at your watering can.

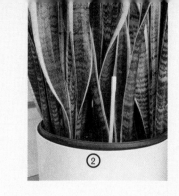

③ **Long-Handled Snips**

Pruning and removing dead leaves is easy when you have scissors with good reach and precision.

④ **Turkey Baster**

When watering larger pots draining into a saucer, you can quickly siphon up overflow with a turkey baster—no need to lift heavy pots. No need to feel helpless as you watch water slowly spilling onto the floor.

⑤ **Damp Paper Towel and Large Sponge**

When leaves collect dust, it can diminish their photosynthesis and gas exchange efficiency. I use a moist paper towel to wipe the surface of the leaf while supporting the back of the leaf with a large sponge. With the added cushioning, I can more thoroughly wipe the leaves.

⑥ **Tank Sprayer**

If you have the inclination to give your plants a shower, using your actual shower can get water everywhere. I find a one- or two-gallon tank sprayer an excellent tool for controlled, high-pressure spraying. The occasional spray can help remove dust from leaves.

⑦ **Small Plastic Tub**

Often you'll need to move a group of plants to a different location to water or repot them. Unless you don't mind walking back and forth multiple times, a small plastic tub is a convenient way to carry multiple plants to your watering station. And repotting plants is easier when you don't need to worry about soil getting all over your floors and tables—the tub helps keep things tidy.

⑧ **Shipping Paper**

When transporting plants in a vehicle, you want to stabilize the base while preventing foliar damage. Packing paper can be crumpled to fit snugly against the base of the pot. In this photo, the paper is also used to keep the foliage from resting against the back of the seat.

⑨ **Mini Sweeper and Dustpan**

A few spills here and there are inevitable. When you don't want or need to grab the vacuum, a small sweeper and dustpan make picking up dirt nice and easy.

⑩ **Cleaning Caddy**

Keep all your tools organized and ready to go using a cleaning caddy.

Part II
House Plant Journal

My most rewarding experiences as an indoor gardener have come from developing an in-depth knowledge of the lives of specific plants. House Plant Journal is a daily photographic record of my plants and what I've learned about them. Although many house-plant books boast of having hundreds of plant profiles, I've decided to share stories of some of the plants that I have most enjoyed growing. I can often show you the changes one of my plants has gone through over several years, so you can imagine how your relationship might progress with the same plant. After all, the most rewarding aspect of plant parenthood is observing your plants as they grow and change!

For each type of plant in the journal section, I describe a survival strategy, suggesting how you might help that plant last as long as possible in low-light situations; and a growth strategy, which tells you what you can expect from a happy plant living in bright indirect light. I also give tips on soil management and notes on a plant's subjective life span—how long you can expect it to maintain a pleasing appearance and what to do when it doesn't.

The selection that follows leans toward the tropical plants that I'm drawn to. Some offer many varieties to try, some have fascinating growth habits, some raise and lower their leaves throughout the day, and still others are a joy to propagate and share.

They range in size from a monster that can take over a room to a tiny vine. Together, they are a world ready for you to explore and learn from.

As your confidence grows, you will inevitably find plants that are not in my collection of greatest hits. If you have copious amounts of direct sun, you may find yourself venturing into the world of cacti and succulents, for example. Remember, the fundamentals of holistic plant care can be applied to any type of plant. The old way of thinking about plant care is that you need specific care information for every plant. The new way is this: Plant care is just minor modifications of the same basic needs.

Dracaena

The growing tip of a dracaena plant emanates from a central stem, or trunk. As new leaves emerge, the older, lower leaves die off. The most common method of cultivation is for the grower to chop back a mature trunk so that three or four new stems can grow from the stump. Sometimes these trunks are planted in a staggered arrangement to produce a pleasing floor plant. Alternatively, one or two plants can grow into a bush. For small spaces, growers may cut a mature cane into several small stumps and plant them individually—plants have the amazing ability to continue growing even when a seemingly large portion of the original plant has been severed. Dormant meristems—regions where there are active cells that can generate new stems—awaken to form new shoots!

Survival strategy

My father-in-law kept a *Dracaena fragrans* alive for what must have been a decade in an upstairs hallway with zero windows. Its leaves were long, narrow, and very dark green. The upstairs lights must have been on for four hours a night at most, and I would estimate the light intensity received by the leaves to be no more than 30 foot-candles. Needless to say, he understood how to care for it. By keeping the soil just barely moist, free from debris, and well aerated, he created conditions where the plant made use of any available soil moisture before root-rot bacteria could take hold. If you think putting a plant in a dark corner will "add some life" to the space, then you need to treat the plant as if it's on life support—because it is.

OPPOSITE: From tallest to shortest: Dracaena marginata, Dracaena deremensis 'Lemon Lime,' and *Dracaena deremensis* 'Warneckii'

Growth strategy

Any space where your dracaena can receive more than 100 foot-candles will allow
it to grow slowly—it's a low-light survivor.
As you increase the light intensity, a few
things will be noticeable: Variegated leaves
will show stronger contrast, fewer lower
leaves will drop (although they'll still drop
eventually!), and the overall height of the
plant will increase noticeably year after
year. A few hours of direct sun is acceptable, but all-day sun exposure may cause
some leaf bleaching.

Soil management

In the right light, dracaenas are tolerant
of both dry soil and saturated soil, but it's
safer to stay on the dry side, which also
means you'll water less frequently—a
bonus for the lazy! As dracaenas tend to
be available as larger plants, you probably
won't be moving them around much for
watering. Regular aeration of the soil will
help with keeping the water penetration
as even as possible. After a year or more,
when you notice roots peeking up on the
soil surface or overall slow growth, you can
either repot, if you have space, or apply a
soil top-dressing.

Subjective life span

Dracaenas are among the longest lasting
plants. They just keep growing taller until
they reach the ceiling, which will likely
take a few years. At this point, you can
cut back the main trunk, and, if the overall
plant is healthy, two or three new stems will
emerge from the cut end. The plant's overall
shape will be drastically altered, but such
is the nature of pruning!

TOP LEFT: The Dracaena 'Torch Cane' fea-
tures interestingly ruffled leaves. Like all
dracaena, its lowest leaves will eventually
become brown and fall off—if your plant
is receiving the right light and you are
watering correctly, then don't worry about
older leaves falling off!

ABOVE: Dracaena cultivation style: staggered trunks with multiple growth tips

Experiences from Dracaena Parenthood

After several years of growth, dracaenas develop true character. Their trunks could probably tell a great story: "Back in the day, before this twisty part . . ." Rotating the plant will set the trunk growing in the direction of the nearest window, so you could theoretically create a nice spiral with regular turns.

The lines, or scars, on the dracaena's trunk indicate where a leaf was attached. In this plant, the spacing between the scars is farther apart

RIGHT: As dracaena leaves age, they will bear the marks of hard work, especially brown tips caused by the build-up of impurities in the water used to moisten the soil, as in this dracaena 'Lemon-Lime.' I don't expect my plants to be flawless sculptures; as long as I'm confident there's enough light and my watering is correct, I know the plant is happy.

in the section indicated by my fingers. By doing a (very rough) calculation of the average leaf-drop rate, I can estimate that this widely spaced section was the top of the plant three years ago. Here's what I think happened: We moved into a new office around that time and put the plant in a bright window. In our old office, the plant had been used for a time as a typical office plant in a sitting area far from any windows, and the growing tip was stretching out for more light, producing leaves more slowly, hence the wider spacing of scars in this area.

ABOVE: If you've been good to your *Dracaena fragrans*, it will shoot up a flower stalk. But be warned, the flowers are pungent and will secrete a sticky sap that may get messy.

Dracaena Foliage Appreciation

In the dracaena genus, you'll find leaves with myriad colors and patterns—deep greens, almost purple, red margins, crinkles, yellow racing stripes, and even a beautiful tricolor of red, green, and white!

Jade Plant

The jade plant *(Crassula ovata)* has long been a favorite of house-plant owners for its plump, teardrop-shaped leaves and the possibility of a treelike structure. New cuttings are all green, but with a few years of bright light, the lower stems develop a woody covering.

Survival strategy

If your daytime high brightness is between 100 and 300 foot-candles, don't expect the jade to grow new leaves as big as the ones it came with. A jade plant sitting far away from a window will grow very slowly and become leggy. At this light level, the plant can only scrape by while holding on to the minimum number of leaves at the growing tips. Older leaves are shed for survival. Be careful about watering—bringing the soil to full saturation at this light level will put the roots at high risk of rot. You would be wise to move the plant to a brighter spot just for a day or two after watering. And because of the long time between waterings, the soil can become quite compacted and should therefore be aerated, which will allow water to penetrate the soil more evenly.

OPPOSITE: Jade plant varieties (clockwise from top): ripple leaf jade, 'Gollum' jade with finger-like leaves, silver jade, the standard plain green, golden jade, and, in the center, the variegated jade

Growth strategy

At 500 foot-candles and higher, including some hours of full sun, your jade plant will grow very happily. You may still find the new growth leggy compared to when you first got the plant, but now, when you prune, there's a better chance you'll get two new stems coming out within a few months. You can easily check how hydrated your jade plants are by gently squeezing a leaf. When it is firm and plump, don't water. Watering should be done when the soil becomes completely dry, but don't wait too long after you see leaves getting wrinkled.

Subjective life span

A jade plant can be enjoyed for several decades in the right light. Don't be afraid to prune it back to encourage branching. You can experiment with propagation by both leaf and stem cuttings, especially if you have a large plant to start with. The most common long-term issue is heavily compacted soil—this can be alleviated by regular aeration and repotting as necessary. Repotting can be done in the spring, once every two years, or even annually if your plant is growing fast. Jades tend to be top-heavy, so be sure to tamp down the soil around the stem and, if necessary, use a stake to keep your plant upright until the root system fills the new container. Use a potting mix with coarse sand and perlite for drainage. You can modify the mix based on your pot material: for a plastic pot (which is more water retentive), use more sand in the mix; for a clay pot (which is more porous), use less sand in the mix.

ABOVE: A small variegated jade plant (left) and several of the standard plants in one pot (right).

Observations from Jade Plant Parenthood

LEFT: A very thirsty jade plant's leaves are floppy and wrinkled. A few days after you soak the soil, the leaves will become plump and regain their firmness.

BELOW: It's especially important to aerate the soil of jade plants because of their preference for prolonged periods of dry soil. Soil can become quite compacted, which will hinder the remoistening process the next time you water.

ABOVE: Don't worry if the oldest leaves turn brown and fall off.

RIGHT: Although jades can handle full sun, some leaves may become scorched and faded.

Varieties of Jade Plants

The sunset jade develops a beautiful orange glow when it is exposed to full sun and is slightly stressed for water.

Pruning and Propagating a Jade Plant

TOP LEFT: You can grow new plants from the cuttings of growing tips or even individual leaves. Let the open scar where the leaf came off the branch scab over (this usually takes a few days), then set it down on moist sand or cactus soil. Here's what you'll get.

ABOVE: If you're looking for a treelike jade plant, you might be better off letting the nursery do all the hard work of training it, but with a bit of effort and strategic pruning, you can do it.

ABOVE: An assortment of stem and leaf cuttings—a jade plant owner will always have a very busy propagation station!

CENTER RIGHT: The newly formed jade plants can be potted in miniature pots. They make excellent gifts for your green-thumbed friends.

BOTTOM RIGHT: Each jade stem will only grow outward, two leaves at a time. The way to encourage branching is to prune the growing tip (which can be propagated). If this is done during the beginning of the growing season and the plant is getting adequate light, two new tips will emerge within a few weeks. A few weeks after a hard pruning (where most of the stems with leaves were cut off), this jade went into hyper leaf-growing mode, producing leaves not only at the outermost node but also at the nodes going back farther on the stem.

Kangaroo Paw Fern

Move aside, Boston and Kimberly Queen ferns, the kangaroo paw fern (*Microsorum diversifolium*) has just as much charm with easier dead-leaf cleanup! Cleaning up dead leaves is an inevitable part of plant parenthood. The kangaroo paw fern's fronds, which grow as a pawlike structure in a single unit, are much easier to clean up when they die than the multitude of leaflets left behind by a Boston or Kimberly Queen fern.

Survival strategy

It's possible to maintain the kangaroo paw fern in a low-light environment—say, around 100 foot-candles. There won't be much growth, and the once-dense foliage will likely thin out as older fronds die off. New fronds will be slow to emerge, and they will probably have a simpler structure—fewer "fingers." You can wait for the soil to be completely dry before watering, as long as you gently aerate it with a chopstick so the water can more evenly penetrate. If you happen to give it a thorough soaking, move it to a window shielded from direct sunlight (as with a sheer white curtain) for a few days, so the plant can have a chance to maintain itself.

Growth strategy

At 200 foot-candles or more (even with some direct sun), a kangaroo paw fern will grow wildly! To support good growth at this light level, you should saturate the soil whenever it becomes partially dry—the fronds will be notice-

ably floppier. Some soil aeration will help to prevent soil compaction. Fertilize when you see new fronds emerging. Hold off if there's a lull in new growth—the plant is resting. In a year or so, you may find that the plant's hairy rhizomes have crawled out of the pot. If just a few are peeking out, you can let the plant be, but if they have taken over the exterior of the pot, then you ought to repot. A peat moss/perlite mixture (5:1) will do

fine. I have yet to divide my own plant, but it seems quite easy to do—just cut through the root ball with a sharp knife and repot the pieces into separate pots. Caution: The hairs on the rhizomes are somewhat prickly!

Observations from Kangaroo Paw Fern Parenthood

① Day 1
My office gave me a plant budget! I found this kangaroo paw fern in an 8-inch basket for a good price. It will live in the office kitchen on one of the large, south-facing windowsills. Since there are many tall buildings nearby, the sun is blocked for most of the daytime hours, which classifies this windowsill as being in "shade." Still, with a good view of the sky, this spot receives an average of 300 foot-candles, with the sun peeking through at odd moments.

② 2 months
Those rhizomes are searching for more soil! The newest fronds (bottom right) are developing from soilless rhizomes!

③ 5 months
Time to repot! It's important to scrape some old soil away from the root ball so new roots can find the new soil sooner.

④ 10 months
After several months in its new 12-inch pot, the fern's new fronds tell me the plant is happy!

⑤ 1 year, 7 months
Here we go again with the searching rhizomes!

⑥ 2 years, 5 months
The pot is now hidden from sight as the fronds growing on the outside have matured. Look back at the 10-month photo and see how the plastic hanger is now drowning in fronds!

Kangaroo Paw Fern Frond Development

①
Here's a young, three-fingered frond; as the overall plant matures, newer fronds will emerge with more "fingers." Fronds do not gain more fingers as they age: This one will always have three fingers.

②
Frond complexity: seven fingers!

③
When fronds start getting little bumps, they have reached fern puberty. In a few weeks, the undersides of these fronds will develop spores from which new plants can be born!

④
Top side of frond: early stages of spore formation.

⑤
Underside of frond: mature spores.

Marimo Moss Ball

The first thing that must be mentioned when introducing Marimo moss balls: They're not technically moss but a form of algae that grows as a sphere. The shape is maintained with the consistent movement of underwater currents. Even in nature, Marimo balls are slow growers, reportedly increasing by about 5 millimeters in diameter per year. So if you want an aquatic ornament that will look mostly the same for years, Marimo balls are a good choice!

Survival strategy
Because these plants live underwater, it's best to keep them completely out of direct sun—some parts of the plant may become brown if exposed to too much sun. They seem to be fine receiving no more than 100 foot-candles as a daily high. The water may become murky and should be changed occasionally—I simply rinse the container, scrubbing with my hand. No soaps or detergents!

Growth strategy
People don't buy Marimo moss balls in the hopes of growing them to a significantly larger size, as they grow quite slowly. It seems that the 300–800 foot-candle range will yield a comfortable rate of growth. Again, avoid direct sun, and change the water whenever you notice it getting murky.

Observations from Marimo Moss Ball Parenthood

Day 1
Received these in the mail—yes, they shipped in a sealed plastic bag and must have been in transit for about a week. I put them in a jar with fresh water.

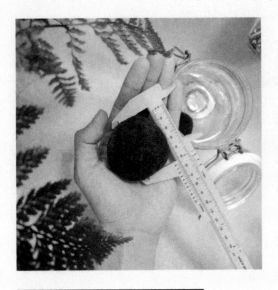

6 months
I wish I had thought to measure my Marimo moss balls when I first got them. Today, the big one measures 55 millimeters in diameter.

Sometimes I let my smaller air plants do their weekly bath with the Marimo moss balls. Since the overall spherical shape is maintained by currents of water, it would seem prudent to give your Marimo moss balls a gentle swirl on a regular basis, though I have not yet seen what would happen if you absolutely never moved them.

1 year
The big ball is now 59 millimeters in diameter. I guess the average of 5 millimeters per year works out!

Money Tree

A money tree *(Pachira aquatica)* is typically raised by braiding four young stems together. This is done primarily because one stem would look rather sparse, with just three or four leaf groupings. When four stems are grouped together, the overall plant has a fuller, treelike appearance

Survival strategy

If you put your newly purchased money tree in a place that gets less than 100 foot-candles, don't expect much new growth, and do expect most of the lower leaves to fall off until you're left with a rather sparse-looking plant. Each stem of the money tree will only hold on to as many leaf groups as the light can provide for. Let the soil become completely dry, aerate it gently, then water. If you don't mind the sparseness, the money tree will survive in low light.

OPPOSITE: I love how a plant develops an individual character after growing in a home environment for an extended time. I've been playing foster parent to a friend's money tree for the past few years. Look at how the branches have grown away from the braided base.

Money Tree

back the stems, even to the point of a stump with no leaves, and it will continue to grow. Money trees are also tolerant of very small pots, but they tend to become top-heavy, so you might want to repot as yours gets large. If you keep it in the same pot, it's a good idea to refresh the soil each year, but you could probably push it to every two years. A money tree can last for many years!

Growth strategy

At 200 foot-candles or more, you'll see growth. Some direct sun is also fine.

Soil management

Money trees seem quite tolerant of all sorts of soil moisture levels, so the least effort would be to water whenever the soil is completely dry. Probe the soil to check the dryness, which will also aerate the roots. You can fertilize as directed whenever you notice new growth occurring.

Subjective life span

Money-tree stems will just keep getting taller. The lowest leaves will always drop off as new ones come in. If you keep the overall plant healthy—getting the right light and watering accordingly—then you can prune

Managing a Money Tree into Maturity

As each stem of a money tree plant will naturally keep growing taller, there will come a time when the weight of the leaves will cause the stems to bend away from the point where the braiding ends. Eventually, you'll have to make a choice . . .

You can tie the stems together against a sturdy metal rod or . . .

You can prune the plant to the height you want. Cut one or two of the stems back to where the braid ends. In a few months, new stems will emerge from this cut. When these grow a few leaves, you can prune back the remaining taller stems. By staggering your pruning, you won't be left with an awkward stump. Notice how new stems emerge from the side of the existing trunks.

Observations of Money Tree Parenthood

It's rare to find a single-stem specimen—this was actually four braided stems, but after months (or even years) in a poorly lit convenience store, only one stem was left. Needless to say, I got a discount on it!

ABOVE LEFT: It would appear that many years ago, the stems decided to go their separate ways!

LEFT: Another friend's money tree, which had always done well in this large north-facing floor-to-ceiling window, was starting to show some curious leaf discoloration and dripping some clear sap. Upon closer inspection, I found that her plant had developed a scale infestation. As there was no backyard where we could spray the plant, I suggested that it might be best to prune back all the branches. Yes, this would leave behind an awkward braided stump, but I could see that the overall plant was healthy.

ABOVE RIGHT: Just two months after cutting back all the stems, new leaves have grown! As long as the plant is healthy, you could keep cutting it right back to the trunk, and new stems will emerge.

Monstera

Attracted by its fascinating leaf patterns, you might adopt one of these without recognizing the "monster" within. Even though it may look well behaved, monstera (*Monstera deliciosa*) is an aggressive vine with very large leaves. The greater the long-term light intensity you can provide, the shorter the inter-leaf spacing will be and the more compact your plant will be, but over time, it will become quite large. Although the popular explanation for the fenestrations (holes and cuts) in the plant's leaves is to resist breakage from strong winds and rain, research has shown that the adaptation is, in fact, a light-capturing optimization strategy—like creating a net with bigger holes to cover more area with less material

Survival strategy

If you must keep your monstera at a distance from a window, it's possible to starve it gracefully and not kill it, but not if you follow instructions for a growing plant. The plant can scrape by with 50–100 foot-candles at the brightest part of the day. Keep the soil on the dry side, and once a week or so loosen it with a chopstick so the roots don't suffocate. When the leaves look really floppy and thin (because they are finally dehydrated), loosen the compacted soil and pour in just enough water to cover the entire surface to a depth of about 2 inches (I'm assuming the pot is at least 8 inches in diameter). If the plant is thirsty enough, you shouldn't get any water running down to the bottom of the pot, where it may linger for weeks. Be prepared to cut off older leaves as they yellow—this is the plant abandoning them as the food reserves are depleted without being replenished.

ABOVE: With the plant up so high, this monstera's light source can only be reflected sunlight for the few hours it shines into the room. Although some would call the plant spindly, it has a certain charm—it seems to say, "This is my shelf. I belong here!"

Monstera

A monstera's leaf pattern is predestined prior to unfurling. Each leaf remains the same as the plant ages. However, if the overall plant is healthy, the next leaf may be bigger and have a more complex pattern of holes and cuts.

New growth will be small and weak, and if the soil is too moist, it may have dark brown tips. Weak plants are also more susceptible to illness, and if your plant was acquired fresh from the nursery, it will grow more spindly as it stretches for light.

Growth strategy

With a nice view of the sky (200 or more foot-candles, and some sun is tolerable), your monstera will happily use up water, so you can bring the soil to saturation whenever it becomes dry to a depth of a few inches.

Soil management

The monstera's soil will eventually be depleted of nutrients, but since monsteras tend to be sold in large pots, you may opt for a top dressing instead of a complete repotting. If you see several new leaves growing, then you can safely apply some fertilizer for the next few weeks. Soil structure is usually pretty good (nice and loose), so just aerate the soil occasionally, maybe every third or fourth watering.

Subjective life span

A monstera can grow for decades in the right environment. Each individual vine will carry about five-to-seven leaves, dropping the oldest leaf as a new one grows. If the tip of the vine is growing too far for your liking, you can simply prune it back to the oldest one or two leaves and give the piece you cut off to a friend to root.

Observations from Monstera Parenthood

Day 1

I responded to a classified ad from someone wanting to sell off this *Monstera deliciosa* because it was becoming too unruly for their small space. Asking price: $10.

7 months

Using a small bamboo trellis from the dollar store, I tied up the vines to give the overall plant a more compact look. Monstera's vines want to grow along some surface, so in a container without a support for them to grow on, the plant will always become unruly and flop over the edges. In this location, the plant gets sunlight filtered through the blinds, measured at 300 foot-candles but only on a clear day. When it's cloudy, the living room gets a dim 50–80 foot-candles. That's a day when a monstera would go hungry.

Monsteras develop aerial roots at nodes along their vines. In nature, these roots can attach themselves to trees. This secures the plant to its support and gives it water and nutrients all along the vines, which may be up to sixty feet long. In your home, it's not necessary for the aerial roots to attach themselves to something like a moss pole or tree trunk. I just hold the vines against the trellis with soft rubber ties, available at most garden centers, and I direct the aerial roots down into the soil.

8 months

It's a bittersweet day when I decide to move my monstera to my church, where she will have a room all to herself. With the front seat pushed all the way forward, my monstera fits right in my Honda Civic. An important change in care routine should be noted: I'm only at my church once a week, and it's far from where I live, which means that I will be forced to water at fixed intervals. But since the light she will be getting is even brighter than in my home, I know that she will be thirsty within a week.

Don't worry, monstera! I'll be seeing you every week. This place has more space for you to grow and better light. Off to the left of this photo is a west-facing windowed door. Late-afternoon sun can be seen hitting the floor, so I've placed the plant slightly farther back so as not to burn the leaves. Maybe when she's older, she'll be able to handle some sun. To the right, a large north-facing window gives perfect "bright indirect light." I measured the light from this area and got over 300 foot-candles. I think monstera will do very well here!

1 year

Leaves are getting more complex.

1 year, 3 months

The monstera has outgrown its bamboo trellis, so I bought a larger metal vegetable trellis. Again, I'm tying the main vines against the trellis and simply directing the aerial roots down into the pot.

2 years

What makes this monstera look so lush and full? There are seven vines in the pot. The growth pattern of Monstera deliciosa is a series of leaves on a single vine. Plants are typically sold as two to three vines in a pot, so even with proper care, the potential "fullness" is limited to the maximum number of leaves that each of those vines can support. Mine happened to have seven vines, so what you're seeing is the combined leaves of those vines.

2 years, 4 months

At this point, my monstera started shedding a number of its oldest leaves. They gradually turned completely yellow; then they were easily removed from the vine. When you understand your growing conditions and their limitations, you can accept life and death. This shedding of older leaves is the reality of nutrient cycling: The plant is pulling the salvageable nutrients from older leaves to make new leaf growth possible. With fertilizer or soil top-dressing, the yellowing of this leaf could have been delayed, but it's unrealistic to believe that it could have been prevented entirely. Accept that the plant must do what it needs for survival.

3 years (OPPOSITE)

Some of the vines have started to grow away from the trellis. I will soon have to adjust them so they can continue to grow upward.

Mother of Thousands (Kalanchoe)

This succulent plant is easily recognized by its spade-shaped leaves with legions of plantlets waiting to be deployed growing along their edges—the plant kingdom's invasion force. If you acquired this plant in a pot, *do not* plant it outdoors, as it is highly invasive in tropical and subtropical regions.

Survival strategy

If you relegate this plant to a low-light area (less than 200 foot-candles), you'll end up with small leaves that don't produce plantlets, which is the main attraction for kalanchoe. Give it as much sky light and sunlight as you can, and you'll get a good showing of plantlets!

Growth strategy

200 foot-candles or more will yield some growth. Give this plant some direct sun and it will live up to its name—well, realistically, maybe just mother of hundreds.

Soil management

With good light, you can water a mother of thousands plant whenever the soil has reached complete dryness. I haven't seen the need to aerate the soil much—an invader's roots are accustomed to poor soil!

Subjective life span

A mother of thousands plant doesn't lend itself to being a "prized specimen" type of plant, due to the sheer volume of plantlets. If you put just one plantlet into its own pot with good cactus soil and give it a sunny location, it will grow to a satisfactory size with many plantlets within a year. As the years go on, the older leaves curl up and drop off the stem, leaving a mess of plantlets growing beneath it to fend for themselves. So the nature of owning a kalanchoe is cyclical—from plantlet, to adult, to propagation of new plantlets.

The stem of the kalanchoe emerges right at the edge of the soil, curves downward, then turns back up.

Observations from Mother of Thousands Parenthood

Day 1

A friend was moving out of town, so I adopted her house plants, including this kalanchoe.

These plantlets are already rooting and ready to invade more soil.

1 year

Look at this army of plantlets! This was only possible because I moved the plant to my office kitchen windowsill, which faces south, but the sun is partially blocked by taller buildings.

2 years

About a year ago, someone at my office thought it would be funny to take a plantlet and stick it into the dracaena's pot. Now this beast is shooting plantlets back into the pot, stealing nutrients from the poor dracaena. After taking this photo, I removed all the babies inside the pot..

OPPOSITE: The natural progression of the kalanchoe is to drop its lowest set of leaves as it continues to grow a new set. All the while, plantlets find their way into neighboring soil—this aloe is not happy with an uninvited guest!

Oxalis

Purple or green *Oxalis triangularis* is commonly available around St. Patrick's Day because of its resemblance to the shamrock or clover (oxalis is sometimes called "false shamrock"). Each stem bears three leaves, and house-plant parents love it that they drop down around the stem at night, like an umbrella closing, and then open each morning. The leaves "know" when to open by remembering the length of time spent in darkness. I once interrupted an oxalis while it was sleeping by exposing a few stems to a bright LED grow light for two hours. Those stems responded by opening to the light. A few hours later, when it was actually morning, the other stems opened, but the ones that got interrupted did not open until later in the morning, when the sun was higher in the sky.

Survival strategy

If you're getting daytime highs of just 100 foot-candles, all the stems your oxalis initially came with will eventually wither away, until you're left with just a pot of soil. Despite this total dieback of foliage, the bulbs are probably still alive. Keep the soil just barely moist, and occasionally aerate it so it's not too compacted. In a few weeks, you should notice new stems emerging. The plant will never achieve the same fullness that it had in the nursery, but at this low light level, you should be happy with two or three stems per bulb.

Growth strategy

If you can get up to 600 foot-candles, the dieback of stems should be offset by new stem growth. Water whenever the soil is partially dry. If your oxalis is getting some direct sun, the soil may reach complete dryness within the same day, causing the stems to be droopy—water immediately and thoroughly! Dead stems can be easily removed by hand once they are completely dried. You can add a liquid fertilizer as directed whenever you see new stems growing.

Subjective life span

Oxalis bulbs can keep producing new stems after dying back, so don't panic when you're left with nothing but a pot of soil. Oxalis grows from a bulb, and it's best to repot once the stems die back or when most of them are on their way to dying off. A regular potting mix of peat with some perlite will do.

ABOVE When the soil is almost completely dry, oxalis leaves will remain slightly closed even during the day: Compare a thirsty oxalis (left) to a well-hydrated plant (right). This is a sign that your plant requires a good soaking immediately.

ABOVE: In lower-light conditions (100–200 foot-candles), many of the stems will likely die back in a few months. After some time while the plant adjusts, it's possible that the bulbs will sprout new stems.

RIGHT: The next set of leaves that grow may not give the same feeling of lushness, but then you can simply change your aesthetic preference to minimalism.

Starting Oxalis from Bulbs

Day 1

You can buy oxalis bulbs and start them anytime. I bought ten on line and distributed them evenly on the soil surface.

Then I covered the bulbs with a thin (quarter-inch) layer of soil. Watered thoroughly and placed in a sunny window.

1 month

1 month since planting: A number of bulbs have put up one stem. Still more to come!

Here we see the early stages of a leaf stem (left) and a flower stalk (right, indicated by my finger). Remember to look closely at the soil level to catch a glimpse of these little ones.

2 months

The leaves have filled out nicely, and we're now treated to some flowers!

Peace Lily

The peace lily grows in a nice, symmetrical splash of leaves, which makes it an excellent stand-alone plant. At the nursery, peace lilies are grown rapidly and given a shot of gibberellic acid, a natural plant hormone that induces flowering. This is how a grower can have flowering peace lilies ready for purchase year-round. In typical home conditions, however, after the initial blooms die off, you're likely going to see two or three blooms occurring several months apart.

Survival strategy

The peace lily is yet another victim of the phrase "thrives in low light." If you want the peace lily to have a chance at life, it needs to see daily highs of at least 50 foot-candles. But at this low level, don't expect much growth. When the soil is mostly dry, peace lilies will wilt dramatically. Only thorough soil drenching will restore the perkiness. Occasionally aerating the soil will help disturb any stale pockets of soil that might otherwise develop, causing root rot.

Growth strategy

Anywhere from 100 to 600 foot-candles will yield good peace-lily growth. Recall

OPPOSITE: The development of a peace lily bloom—the entire process takes a few weeks.

that soil moisture usage becomes more rapid with greater light intensity, so when you expose the peace lily to even brighter conditions (800 foot-candles up to full sun), the plant will get to the point of wilting within a few days, at which point you will need to immediately water it thoroughly to prevent permanent damage. So giving the peace lily light in the range of 100–600 foot-candles will balance good growth with comfortable watering frequency.

Subjective life span

Some plant parents may become bored with the peace lily once the initial blooms fade, but for those who understand indirect light and water accordingly, the peace lily will reward them with blooms every few months. Be ready to cut off yellowed leaves as new ones grow.

ABOVE: Giving a wilting peace lily an immediate soaking will get it to perk back up, but don't make a habit of letting it get to this wilted state—roots can be permanently damaged, causing the corresponding leaves to not regain their spring.

RIGHT: Heavy application of gibberellic acid can sometimes lead to irregularities in peace lily blooms—such as multiple flowers growing from the same stem (right). Compare this with a regular peace lily bloom (left).

Observations from Peace Lily Parenthood

A large variegated peace lily enjoying filtered light—sun shining through a white sheer curtain.

The variegated peace lily has lovely white splashes and a rough textured leaf.

Spotting a bloom is one of the most exciting parts of peace lily parenthood. It's said that a peace lily is more likely to bloom when it is slightly pot-bound. This makes sense from an evolutionary standpoint—before the emergence of a new leaf, the plant assesses whether it is the right time to reproduce by seed. If the roots sense they are a bit crowded, then it would be worthwhile to spread new life by way of seed, as opposed to growing more leaves at the current site.

New growth emerges as a rolled leaf emanating from the side of a previous leaf. When this new leaf has grown tall enough to reveal its stem, you should keep an eye out for the flower bump.

Cut off spent blooms at the stem, just above where the bloom emerges from the leaf sheath.

Once these older leaves have become completely yellow, simply cut them off—as long as you are providing the best light you can and watering accordingly, removing older yellowed leaves is a normal part of plant parenthood.

OPPOSITE

The same peace lily after a good post-blooming maintenance session.

Blooms remain a nice white for several weeks up to a couple of months, but they'll all eventually fade to green or brown. At this time, you may find the overall plant looks unsightly, so cut off the spent blooms and enjoy the foliage until the next round of blooming.

If your peace lily was fresh from the nursery, you may notice many older leaves yellowing and/or developing brown spots as the plant adjusts to your home environment.

Philodendron Vines

Philodendrons always work in hanging baskets. Here's a beautiful specimen of philodendron silver (*Scindapsus pictus*).

Philodendron is the common name used for a group of species that are quite similar; included among the vining philodendrons are *Scindapsus pictus*, *Philodendron hederaceum* 'Brasil,' *Philodendron hederaceum*, and *Philodendron hederaceum micans*. Vining philodendrons look very much like pothos and require the same care.

Survival strategy

Philodendron vines can maintain a pleasing look with minimal light (around 50 foot-candles), but that's all they'll be doing—holding on for dear life. You can try keeping the soil barely and evenly moist with regular soil aeration to prevent stale pockets of moisture from festering.

Growth strategy

From 100 to 300 foot-candles, you'll get some vine growth. Above 300 up to about 800 foot-candles, variegation will be more pronounced. However, when philodendrons are exposed to direct sun for more than an hour or two, darker leaves may fade, giving them a bleached look. It is therefore best to shield the plant with a white sheer curtain if the sun shines directly into your window for several hours on a clear day.

Soil management

Assuming adequate light, keep the soil evenly moist for strong growth. When the soil is almost completely dry, you'll notice that the leaves become floppy and dull. This should be immediately remedied by some soil aeration to loosen up the dry pockets, followed by bringing the soil to saturation. Leaves should become perky again in a day or two. You can use a liquid fertilizer as directed when you notice vines putting out new leaves.

Subjective life span

After a year or two, if your plant has been adjusting well, you might end up with some bare spots near the soil, as the outer parts of the vine remain lush. Just as with pothos, you can take cuttings, root them, and transplant them back into the main pot or start several smaller planters. Philodendrons are excellent long-term house plants.

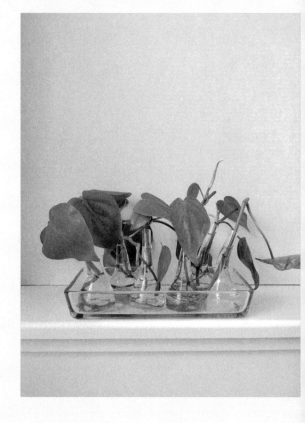

TOP LEFT: Philodendron vines will just keep getting longer. They can be fixed to the wall with help from some small wall hooks, creating the effect of a wildly growing space. They may even attach themselves to your wall.

LEFT: Bleached leaves: These vines get direct sun for 3 to 4 hours in the summer, which is a bit too much for philodendrons. Left: a sunburned leaf appears faded while normal leaves (center and right) have deeper greens.

ABOVE: Heartleaf philodendron cuttings: Once rooted, they can go back into the original pot for a fuller look or they can be transplanted into small pots and given to friends.

Philodendron Versus Pothos

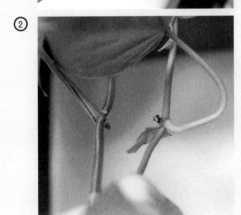

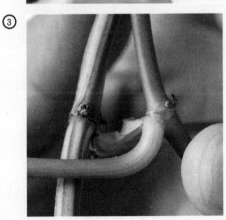

① Growing tip

On a pothos (left), the new leaf and its stem are roughly the same color as the rest of the plant, and the growing tip is the leaf itself. The growing tip of a philodendron (right) has a reddish color, and its main vine extends while the previous leaf continues to unfurl.

② Left sheath

The pothos sheath (left) is always attached to the petiole (the stalk that connects the leaf to the main vine) while a philodendron's sheath (right) hangs loose and may eventually fall off.

③ Aerial root nub and vine

Pothos (left) usually has one bigger, woody root nub with other smaller ones, and the node can be prickly! The vine has a grooved, rougher surface. The philodendron root nubs (right) are smaller and not quite as spiky. The vine is smoother on a philodendron.

Varieties of Vining Philodendrons

ABOVE All of these variegated leaves came from the same philodendron 'Brasil' plant! Note: No leaves were harmed in the making of this image.

OPPOSITE TOP LEFT Commonly known as "heartleaf philodendron," Philodendron hederaceum produces a lovely green leaf and prolific vines that are easy to propagate.

OPPOSITE TOP RIGHT Philodendron silver (*Scindapsus pictus*) has a lovely pattern of silver flecks that glitter in bright light. Some people call this plant satin pothos, but I prefer to reserve the common name pothos for plants in the Epipremnum genus. Like pothos, it has green stems instead of reddish ones.

OPPOSITE BOTTOM LEFT Philodendron 'Brasil' is a cultivar of heartleaf philodendron that sports a yellow stripe with a seemingly random pattern.

OPPOSITE BOTTOM RIGHT Velvet leaf philodendron (Philodendron hederaceum micans) lives up to its name. This is a newly potted set of cuttings. Here's hoping it will grow into some long vines.

Pilea

Pilea peperomioides is one of the most desired house plants. As it became popular, commercial growers scrambled to get stock, and individuals with some space and good light were selling individual plants in classified ads for up to $80 for a small 4-inch pot! Fortunately, a healthy plant will put out pups (little baby versions of itself) in a relatively short time, so you could easily trade for one among a group of plant enthusiasts (which is how I acquired mine).

Survival strategy

If you fell into the trap of wanting to put this plant on display on a shelf far away from any windows, be prepared to pick up dead foliage as older leaves become yellow and fall off. Anything less than a daily high of 150 foot-candles will cause the plant to adjust by aborting older leaves. In a few months, if the plant didn't succumb to root rot because its soil stayed moist for too long, you would be left with no more than two to three leaves growing very slowly at the top of a bare stem, and the constant yellowing and dying off of older leaves might cause you to worry. It's just typical adjustment to low light. The risk of root rot can be mitigated somewhat with soil aeration.

Growth strategy

Give pilea a nice view of the sky and even a couple of hours of sun, and it will grow nicely. Older leaves will still become yellow and fall off, but the overall plant will remain lush, with leaves growing as large as 4 inches in diameter. When pilea is growing with

ABOVE: A wonderfully mature pilea with a bent stem—it has character.

more than 200 foot-candles, it tends to use up soil moisture within a few days. Keep the soil evenly moist and well aerated during growth. A special note on aeration—be very careful, as you do not want to damage the underground runners that will eventually become pups.

Subjective life span

A healthy pilea plant can send up six to eight pups within the first year of ownership. You will then have your hands full with pup separation and transplanting. At this time, the original mother plant will start looking somewhat tired, having dropped several of her oldest leaves. If you're brave, you can experiment with cutting the mother plant's main stem and getting it to root, while the stump continues to produce pups.

TOP: Some homegrown Pilea peperomioides ready to hit the classified ads

ABOVE: With good light, a pilea will produce many pups, sometimes within a few months of the mother plant becoming established.

Observations from Pilea Parenthood

Day 1

I finally got my hands on a *Pilea peperomioides*! A local plant lover posted one of her pups for trade on a Facebook group, and I just happened to have the neon pothos she was looking for.

4 months

A few new leaves have grown after the first repotting, from a 2-inch pot up to this 3½-inch pot. The soil is the usual: peat moss with added perlite.

8 months

Another pot graduation! Now we're up to a 5-inch nursery pot. During this repotting session, I found a nice surprise . . .

The first pup!

10 months

Since the repotting, two pups have been growing strong. At this size, they are ready to be separated into their own pots.

1 year

Upon removing the mother plant from its pot, I found some younger pups in earlier stages of development and two more runners under the soil, looking for light, so they too can become pups. If this runner crawling along the bottom of the pot had found a drainage hole, it would have developed into a pup underneath the pot!

Using a sharp, clean knife, cut the connection between the mother and pup at the root/soil level.

A few of the separated pups, ready to be potted!

The standard potting procedure: Appropriately sized nursery pots lined with landscape fabric.

After gently tamping down the soil to ensure it is firmly around the entire root ball, I water the soil thoroughly. The watering action further settles the soil around the roots.

When repotting the mother plant, I carefully reoriented the runner so that it would eventually find its way to the soil surface.

1 year, 1 month

A month has passed since the repotting. The runner has emerged and successfully developed its first set of leaves! In a few more months, I'll need to do the separation procedure again.

1 year, 3 months

The mother pilea (back left) and her firstborn (front left). The three younger siblings (right), which have been raised with the grow light. Notice the flatness of the leaves.

Light and Its Effect on Pilea Growth

Day 1

Upon separating and transplanting the first round of babies, I was curious to see if there would be any noticeable differences between growing a young pilea under natural light (under my skylight) and using a LED grow light. Here's my assessment of the light characteristics:

Day 30

The pilea grown under natural light (left), which we would call "low light" at best, has quite a bit more doming of leaves. The pilea grown under the grow light (right) has the desired flatter leaves.

Day 92

Although the days are becoming longer, the natural-light pilea (left) still exhibits more doming of leaves than the pilea grown under the grow light (right).

TOP VIEW: The pilea grown under the grow light (right) has more compact stems, as they did not need to reach farther for stronger light.

NATURAL LIGHT

Duration: Intensity rises and falls with the day length. Since this experiment was done in the winter, day length at my latitude was around 9 hours.
Intensity: The sun never crossed into view, so the light was exclusively from the sky. The intensity peaked on average at 200 foot-candles.

GROW LIGHT

Duration: I set the timer to 12 hours on and 12 hours off.
Intensity: The grow light was adjusted to sit at a height of about 6 inches away from the tallest leaf. At this distance, the light intensity reading was 800 foot-candles.

Ponytail Palm

The most widely available species of the genus Beaucarnea is *Beaucarnea recurvata*, commonly called ponytail palm, with long leaves that sometimes resemble gently curled hair. Cultivators prune a young tree to a stump, which stimulates new stems to sprout, creating the look of a miniature palm tree.

Survival strategy

If you want to use this plant purely for décor, it will stay acceptably nice with as low as 50 foot-candles. Once a month, you can drench the soil and leave it right up against a window for a week, so the plant can produce some carbohydrates before its low-light fasting time. For the rest of the time, the soil should be kept bone dry.

Growth strategy

At 200 foot-candles or more, the leaves will continue to get longer. With some sun, you may even see new sets of leaves sprouting from lower points on the trunk. Ponytail palms are usually potted in a fast-draining cactus mix—less peat moss, more coarse sand, and sometimes with some bark chips. Whenever the soil has been completely dry for a week or more, you can give it a thorough soaking. The correct potting mix will not hold too much moisture

OPPOSITE: Three styles of Beaucarnea: Ponytail palm (left), with multiple leaf sets; very young sprouts (center); and *Beaucarnea stricta* (right), which tends to grow straighter and with broader leaves.

anyway, so don't worry when soaking, as most of the water will drain away.

Subjective life span

A ponytail palm can last for many years, although the only growth you may notice is the elongation of its leaves. In a home environment, you're not likely to see an increase in trunk girth—let the nursery take care of that before you purchase the plant.

ABOVE: Other than the common *recurvata* "mini palm tree" style of cultivation, you can sometimes find very young sprouts—a small bulb with a set of grasslike leaves.

Observations from Ponytail Palm Parenthood

TOP LEFT: A friend kept his ponytail palm surviving through the winter by using a simple grow light setup—it was really more of a life-support system until he could get the plant back outside in the spring/summer.

TOP RIGHT: A typical ponytail palm has multiple points of growth occurring on a thick stump.

BOTTOM LEFT: The usual growth structure of the Beaucarnea is a single set of leaves growing from the tip of the trunk, as in this photo. If this trunk is cut, the overall structure will change into multiple leaf sets emerging from several growth points.

ABOVE: Ponytail palm leaves can grow into a beautifully spiraling shape.

Pothos

Although it is considered invasive in tropical regions, pothos (*Epipremnum aureum*), like philodendron, deserves a place in any collection of house plants. The variegated varieties make up what I like to call the Pothos Fab Four: 'Marble Queen,' 'Golden,' "N'joy,' and 'Neon.' Sometimes a 'Golden' or' Marble Queen' pothos may start putting out pure green leaves, which is undesirable if you're a commercial grower but interesting for a plant parent—you can clip off this pure green vine to create a separate plant of all pure green leaves!

Survival strategy

Pothos can survive in areas receiving no more than 50 foot-candles, but be prepared for a long adjustment period where there will be little to no growth. Bringing the soil to maximum saturation won't kill the pothos at first, but if you keep it moist, in a few months you might find a fungal infection that causes black spots to form in the middle of leaves. This can be avoided with regular soil aeration.

Growth strategy

From 100 to 300 foot-candles, you'll get good pothos growth. Above that, variegation will be more pronounced. If you start exposing the pothos to direct sun, you may notice some fading of the green after some weeks—it's probably best to block direct sun with a sheer

OPPOSITE: Pothos Fab Four (clockwise from top): 'Marble Queen,' 'Golden,' "N'joy,' and 'Neon.'

curtain. Keep the soil evenly moist, which will give the leaves a perky bounce as you pat them. If the plant starts to wilt, do a quick pour all around the soil surface. When the plant is growing, you can use any fertilizer as directed. Pothos roots will grow quickly, and you should watch out for when they begin to emerge from the pot's drainage holes. That's a good sign that a larger pot is necessary. Another is when your plant has been growing steadily for several months and, suddenly, numerous leaves, sometimes on the same vine, become yellow and fall off. This could mean the roots of that vine have rotted. Repotting the plant will effectively reset the soil nutrients and structure.

Subjective life span

The main concern for long-term satisfaction with pothos is the plant's oldest leaves starting to yellow and fall off, which can be caused by any number of factors, including loss of soil nutrients or root damage from a dry spell. Fortunately, propagation by stem cuttings is very easy, so you can transplant rooted cuttings back into the soil. However, if you repot your plant and refresh the soil in a timely manner, you'll have it for a long time.

ABOVE: Bringing life to a dark corner? More like sentencing a plant to a slow death by starvation.

Pothos Propagation

Each pothos vine only grows in one way—longer! So when a vine reaches the floor and you're not into the jungle look, you can simply cut it with clean, sharp pruning shears, preferably closer to the older leaf. In time, a new growing tip will emerge, and the vine will continue its quest in getting longer. With the healthy leaves you cut off, you can easily propagate more plants. Pothos is a great plant for learning how to propagate, because it roots under almost any conditions. Thanks to its rapid growth (assuming it's in good light), you can start to make new plants every few months. Here are some jade pothos cuttings rooting in water.

Each cutting should have one leaf, one stem, and one segment of the main vine. You'll see a brown root node where the stem meets the main vine; this is where new roots will emerge. To get a lot of plants quickly, I bundle a few cuttings together (five to seven) with a soft rubber tie and put them in a glass of water in an area where they will not receive direct sun. As the days go by, I make sure the water remains clear and remove cuttings that turn yellow or brown (this doesn't happen very often). In a few weeks, white roots are growing from the node, and as soon as I see roots emerging from all cuttings, I transplant them in into a small (4-inch) nursery pot

with any standard potting mix. The tie will assist in keeping the stems upright while the roots are establishing themselves. In a few weeks, I remove the tie, as the stems are standing upright on their own. The new plants come in handy if the mother plant has bare stems near the soil that I want to conceal.

Observations from Pothos Parenthood

GUTTATION

The water transport mechanism in the pothos is so efficient that excess water can collect at the leaf tips after a thorough watering. Is this a sign that you're "overwatering"? No, not if your plant is growing!

THE TOTEM

An alternative way of cultivating pothos is to let the vines grow onto a rough surface that can hold a bit of moisture, such as bark or a moss pole. Each leaf will become larger than its predecessor. While this may be tempting to try, your success rate will depend on whether you can provide enough light and your ability to keep the rough surface irrigated.

GOLDEN POTHOS

In nature—with heat, humidity, and plenty of rain—a pothos can reach an impressive size that many wouldn't even recognize. This is a 'Golden' pothos!

Prayer Plant

Each night, *Maranta leuconeura*'s leaves fold up to resemble hands in prayer, hence its common name. The leaves grow at the ends of bent stems that drape over the edge of the pot, which is why prayer plants are often sold as hanging baskets. Some people tie the vines to vertically positioned stakes, but I find this looks awkward. Younger vines will occasionally send out small flowers from a spike—the flowers are less interesting than the leaves!

Survival strategy

Prayer plants can live in low light, but that doesn't mean they can survive in a dark corner. It means they can tolerate down to 50 foot-candles as the daytime high. If you're just barely keeping the soil evenly moist, as you would in a low-light situation, then there will come a point when the entire plant goes limp because a significant portion of its root system is damaged from dry pockets. When this happens, be sure to give the soil a gentle aeration and a thorough soaking.

Growth strategy

New leaves will steadily emerge when the daily light levels reach 200 foot-candles. Above 300 up to about 800 foot-candles, variegation will be more

OPPOSITE: A green prayer plant (left) and a *Calathea lancifolia* (right): Both fold up during the night. Calatheas are similar to prayer plants in their care needs and are often grown alongside them.

pronounced. An hour or two of direct sun is tolerable, but the plant should not be in direct sun for an entire day.

Soil management

Given adequate light, keep the soil evenly moist for strong growth. If the soil becomes mostly dry, the entire plant will go limp. This should be immediately remedied by some soil aeration to loosen up the dry pockets, followed by bringing the soil to saturation. Leaves should become perky again in a day or two. You can use a liquid fertilizer as directed when you notice new leaves.

Subjective life span

If the prayer plant has one weakness, it's pests. Perhaps it is a combination of the stem and leaf structures having nooks and crannies where pests can hide and the plant sap being particularly attractive. All of my prayer plants have had to be discarded within a year or so because of an unmanageable infestation.

Propagating Prayer Plants

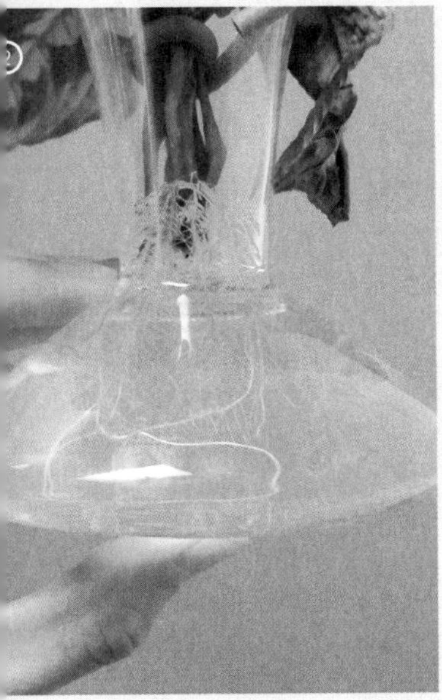

①

A few maranta stems freshly cut and submerged in water for rooting.

②

Ensure that the cut ends are submerged in the water. Roots will emerge from the nodes—the bumps at the bent part of the stems.

③ 2 months later

Cuttings can be transplanted as soon as the roots are half an inch long, but because they are submerged in water, you can leave them until you have time to transplant them. Note that some cuttings might die along the way—that's life!

④

As the older leaves yellow, the inner parts of the vine look bare, and the once-bushy maranta now looks quite sad. I'd suggest taking cuttings while the plant is bushy, so when it eventually gets to looking bare, you'll have some rooted cuttings ready to fill in the pot. Here, I'm transplanting a rooted stem cutting into soil. This will fill in the pot.

It's All About the Leaves

ABOVE: New leaves emerge like rolls of paper. Look at the lovely pattern of dark and light flecks on this green prayer plant, *Maranta leuconeura* var. *'kerchoveana.'*

TOP RIGHT: New leaves on the red-veined prayer plant (*Maranta leuconeura* var. *'erythrophylla'*) resemble rolls of purple wrapping paper!

RIGHT: Marantas can sometimes put out some interesting leaf colors!

Observations from Prayer Plant Parenthood

8 months

The plant doesn't live here; it's just waiting for its turn in the shower where I can water it thoroughly without worrying about getting water all over my floors.

10 months

Yellowing leaves popping up here and there will be removed once they are fully turned.

An older leaf yellowing is the plant trying to recycle the nutrients that can be salvaged, such as nitrogen, phosphorous, and potassium. If you don't find it too unsightly, it's best to let these leaves become fully yellow before cutting them off.

Removing yellowed leaves is a normal part of plant parenthood.

1 year, 3 months

A thrips infestation! Lucky for me that I propagated cuttings and started some new plants.
Thrips will strip away the protective coating on stems and leaves.

The undersides of prayer plants seem to make ideal homes for plant pests like thrips (seen here), spider mites, or scale. Not wanting to spread the infestation to other plants, I decided it would be best to discard the plant. I'll buy another basket if I come across a nice specimen.

Rabbit's Foot Fern

The rabbit's foot fern (*Davallia fejeensis*) has more intricate foliage than a Boston fern, and its rhizomes are fascinating (although scary for some—there's a reason it's mistakenly called "tarantula fern"). The fronds of this fern don't dry up in a mess of leaves; instead, they gradually turn yellow and fall off as one piece.

Survival strategy

This fern seems to be able to maintain itself with low light hovering around 100 foot-candles. The plant won't grow much and will likely thin out, losing a number of fronds, but it should remain lush enough to keep you interested. While it can tolerate completely dry soil, you'll need to gently loosen it with a chopstick before watering, or else the compacted pockets will never get wet. Just be careful not to pierce the rhizomes.

Growth strategy

With 200 or more foot-candles, the frond turnover should be slower. You can comfortably bring the soil to saturation whenever it becomes partially dry. The soil should be aerated occasionally. A general-purpose fertilizer will do whenever you find the plant is in growing mode, when several new fronds are unfurling.

Subjective life span

If you provide it with enough light, the rhizomes of this fern may completely surround its container in a few years. At this point, you can divide the entire plant or simply cut off a few rhizomes and transplant them into new soil.

Rhizomes

OPPOSITE: As they mature, they will eventually become a lighter green, like the rest of the mature fronds.

LEFT: In ferns, the rhizome is simply a horizontal root stem that grows out from the mother plant above the soil and is capable of sending out new roots and new fronds, generating a new plant. The more established rhizomes of the rabbit's foot fern have light-brown "fur," while the new growing tips are white with a slight green tint.

RIGHT: Note the emergence of new fronds from the hairy rhizomes: They are initially a dark brownish green—don't mistake them as being sick!

Repotting a Rabbit's Foot Fern

I put this rabbit foot's fern into a cachepot for now until I can decide on a planter that will accentuate its most interesting feature—the furry rhizomes!

A year later, I found an interesting glass container for my rabbit's foot fern. After removing some of the old soil, I'll use sphagnum moss to line the inside of the container, as it doesn't have drainage holes.

Any time you transplant, it's a good idea to loosen some of the old soil from the root ball so that the roots can more easily explore the new soil.

OPPOSITE: Eight months since repotting: Living in my bathroom, this plant receives a daily high of around 200 foot-candles. At this light level, I notice the sphagnum moss becomes completely dry in approximately a week's time. Because the container lacks drainage holes, I slowly pour in a volume of water equivalent to a quarter or a third of the total volume of sphagnum moss. This will adequately moisten the entire volume of moss.

Lining the container with sphagnum moss.

Inserting the root ball into the pocket of sphagnum moss.

Snake Plant

The sansevieria genus, commonly called the snake plant, represents a kind of win-win house plant. Snake plants prefer dry soil, which translates to low watering frequency. There are myriad species available to collect, so there's the excitement of rarity with the robustness of a hardy plant!

Survival strategy

Snake plants are often relegated to windowless corners because people started labelling them as a "thrives in low light" kind of plant. I prefer to describe it as: starves gracefully at less than 50 foot-candles. If this is the case in your home, you should just barely moisten the soil only after long periods (weeks) of being bone dry. If you're up for it, you can give the soil a complete soaking and then put the plant near a window getting 300 or more foot-candles. Leave it there for a week so it can actually do some growing before you force it to starve again.

OPPOSITE: A snake plant family portrait!

Growth strategy

Giving snake plants enough light to grow is easy because of the wide range of acceptable light intensities. They will be happy with as low as 100 foot-candles and as high as 1,000 foot-candles. In full sun (meaning exposed to direct sun for more than four hours), however, the greenness may start fading. Thus, bright indirect light is preferred.

Soil management

A snake plant stores most of its water in its thick leaves, so the soil can be left bone dry between waterings. When you do water, it's a good idea to gently aerate the soil to ensure that water penetrates as evenly as possible. If the snake plant leaves appear wrinkly, you should give the soil a good soaking immediately. Because snake plants can handle prolonged dry soil, it tends to form clumps that are difficult to remoisten. If the soil hasn't been changed in over a year, it might be a good idea to repot. Use any well-draining mix—typically potting soil with coarse sand added or premade "cactus" mix will suffice.

Subjective life span

A nursery-grown snake plant (for example, the usual tall kind, *Sansevieria trifasciata* 'Laurentii') will have strong, broad leaves, like swords. After a year or two, you may notice that new leaves will not be as wide if your plant has been living in sub 100 foot-candle light. After several years, some of the oldest leaves will flop over and bend permanently, even if you give the soil a good soaking. If you find that unsightly, you can cut off those leaves.

TOP LEFT: Even a few feet away from a north-facing window, the light drops off significantly—this snake plant never gets much more than 80 foot-candles of light. While it won't grow much, it will manage to "look alive" for many months.

TOP RIGHT: One year later, I'm still collecting more species and branching out into different container styles.

LEFT: Snake plants have been popular house plants ever since plants have been brought into the home. Some varieties of snake plant could be considered "vintage cultivars," as they are not currently commercially grown. Don't be fooled by the mid-century modern furniture, though; this photo was not taken in the 1950s!

A Snake Plant for the Office

A *Sansevieria trifasciata* destined to be an office plant. The Ikea outer pot didn't quite fit the standard nursery pot.

Day 21

New growth emerges as a rosette. In a year or so, all of this soil surface will be brimming with new snake plant leaves!

New snake plant leaves emanate from underground runners—they push horizontally through the soil until they encounter a barrier or until they've traveled sufficiently to start growing upward.

3 months

A deep windowsill made the ideal home for the snake plant—a clear view of the sky! Although this window faces south, there are many tall buildings that block the sun for most of the colder months, when the noontime sun is lower.

2 years

When I was given a lovely new planter, I decided it should be home to the office snake plant. To make it fit nicely, I had to cut back part of the rim of the plastic nursery pot.

3 years

3 years—and what's this? A flower stalk!

The office snake plant is looking more stylish in its new planter. Living in this windowsill has certainly encouraged lots of growth, filling up the pot with leaves. I wonder if I'll ever see flowers.

Snake plant flowers can be quite fragrant. Fortunately, no one's desk is too close to the plant.

Propagating Snake Plants

① After about a year of growing at a mature size, snake plants will send up offshoots, which can be separated once they have reached about a third of the size of the mother plant.

② A mother and baby snake plant— these bird's nest snake plants grow as a compact rosette.

③ Bird's nest snake plants in various stages of development. Another method of propagation is leaf cutting, where the cut end of a leaf is placed in water or, more commonly, moist sand. After some time (it could be months), a new rosette will emerge. I've never done this type of propagation, since snake plants grow so slowly and most are cheaply and readily available at my local nurseries.

④ Leaves grown at the nursery are broad, stiff, and swordlike. After a year or so, you'll notice the new leaves grow out from rosettes that emerge from the soil. This pale green variety is called 'Moonshine.'

Whale Fin Snake Plant

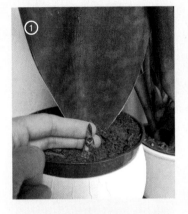

① **Day 1**
Sansevieria masoniana, or whale fin snake plant, is fascinating to watch grow. When they say that snake plants are slow growers, it doesn't mean that a new leaf takes a long time to develop. It means that there are month-long periods when nothing seems to be happening. I noticed this spike emerge only a week after bringing the plant home—it must have been the right time!

② **6 days later**
The new leaf has doubled in height from two fingers to four fingers tall.

③ **20 days later**
Now it's about a third the height of its mother.

④ **27 days later**
The baby has reached halfway!

⑤ **40 days later**
In case you're wondering, the snake plant on the left is called *Sansevieria* trifasciata 'Bantel's Sensation.'

⑥ **64 days later**
I love the "brand-new" look of the newly unfurled leaf—such a beautiful pattern! You could separate them to create two potted single-leaf specimens, but I think they look nice together—more whale-fin-like!

Staghorn Fern

Like all members of the genus Platycerium, the staghorn fern (*Platycerium bifurcatum*) has two main parts: the fertile fronds, which can be dangling or upright, like hands reaching up for the sky, and the shield frond, or sterile frond, which grows around the base, forming a dome that covers the surface upon which the plant rests. When the plant matures in favorable conditions, the underside of the fertile fronds develop deep brown patches—these are the spores. And don't fret about the shield frond becoming brown—the plant tends to put out a new one every few months during its growing season.

Survival strategy

I'm going to quote Michael Jackson here: "If you can't feed your baby, then don't have a baby." A mounted staghorn fern will slowly die in typical "low light" conditions, that is, less than 100 foot-candles. Avoid the temptation to proudly mount one on the wall above your couch, away from any windows.

Growth strategy

Give it 300 foot-candles or more and you'll enjoy a happy staghorn fern. A large window or a skylight is ideal, with daytime highs of 500–600 foot-candles. The plant will want to see as much of the open sky as possible but be protected from direct sun—one or two hours of direct sun is tolerable.

Staghorns will grow perfectly fine in a pot, but the more interesting way to appreciate a specimen is when it is mounted.

LEFT: A fresh batch of staghorn ferns—perhaps I shall adopt one and mount it (instructions to follow).

BELOW: An example of a potted staghorn fern (on a tall pedestal, where it belongs!)

Soil management

In a pot, the staghorn fern will probably come in typical tropical plant soil (peat moss, perlite, maybe compost). Keep it aerated and evenly moist. When the plant is mounted on a board (instructions to follow) in a bed of sphagnum moss, the increased moisture-retention ability of the moss as compared to soil is counterbalanced by the increased rate of evaporation, since more of the planting medium is exposed to air. You can easily feel the moss to judge moisture—once the outer parts are crispy, it's time to resoak the moss. If you wait longer—and you shouldn't— the whole mound will feel like a dry sponge. Prior to watering, it's helpful to loosen the sphagnum moss. You'll have to be gentle but firm, as the moss tends to harden and become quite compacted. Some plant-care directions say to soak the entire board in a bathtub, but that's too much of a hassle and really not necessary. If the mound of moss is small, you can simply lay the plant in a large sink or bathtub and pour water into the sphagnum moss until it is completely soaked through. Leave the plant for a few hours to let the excess water drip away, then put it back in its growing position. Whether or not you wet the fronds doesn't really matter; what matters is that the planting medium should be evenly moistened. For my own plant, I run it under the shower at night and leave it to drip-dry overnight. By the following morning, the entire board can be put back up on the wall. Fertilize whenever you see new fronds growing.

Subjective life span

Staghorn ferns are long-lived, but there is a leaf progression of loss and replacement. On older fertile fronds, some yellowing begins somewhere in the middle of the leaf, then spreads to the rest of it. At this time, you should be able to pull it off from the base of the plant. After three years of my own plant growing under a skylight, I'd say it has stabilized to growing three to five new fertile fronds while losing three to five old ones each year. The sterile frond (or shield frond) grows to cover the base of the plant and is easily bruised. By the time this shield frond covers the entire base, it will begin to turn brown, which is natural. In favorable conditions, a staghorn fern will grow pups that you can either let grow together as a cluster or separate by root division.

Observations from Staghorn Fern Parenthood

Day 1

Bought this lovely stag-
horn fern in a 6-inch pot.
The shield frond was a bit
damaged, but so were all the
other specimens. I picked out
all these stowaway seedlings.

Let the mounting begin! Here's a description of my materials:

Mounting board: The hardware store sells pine project boards for shelf-making. I cut one to size and treated it with a non-toxic varnish, thinking that it would protect the board from the high moisture of the sphagnum moss.

Landscape fabric: I felt that a barrier between the board and the sphagnum moss would be good to have.

Plastic mesh: I stapled pieces to the board to make little baskets. I probably should have made them a bit bigger.

Sphagnum moss: From my research, you really have to pack this in tightly around the staghorn's roots.

Heavy-duty frame-mounting hardware: Soon, I'll mount the hanging wire on the board and find a place to hang this plant trophy!

Regardless of your mounting process, you will damage the existing shield frond, so don't get hung up on it.

As I unpotted the plant, my suspicions were confirmed—I had two plants!

I created pockets using plastic mesh stapled to a wooden board, which, in retrospect, wasn't the best mounting method—more on that later. I put a layer of landscape fabric between the plastic and the wood. Looking at the size of the pockets, I knew I had to remove a lot of the old potting medium from around the roots in order to get the mound of sphagnum moss and the plant to fit. I packed the moss as tightly as I could around the roots and closed the pocket around the plant.

Mounted! I haven't hung it on the wall yet, so for now, it lives on top of the bathroom shelf, getting light from the skylight. I water it by resting it on this bucket (with holes in the lid) and completely soaking the sphagnum moss each time it becomes almost completely dry. Sphagnum moss is very much like a sponge: When it's dry, it's hard and flaky.

3 months

The first sign of the new shield frond!

5 months

A second shield frond has started to grow!

At this size, the most convenient way to water was to put the entire board into the shower stall and shower it with tepid water. I would leave the plant to drip-dry in the shower overnight, then place it back on the wall the next day.

4 months

Remember how I said using the plastic mesh wasn't the best idea? It's because of how the shield frond grows tightly around its planting mound—it eventually pushed itself against the mesh. I did a little operating to remove pieces of the mesh, but the shield frond bruises like a peach! Still, the scars give the plant more character.

1 year since mounting

The board has finally been mounted to the wall. I used standard picture-hanging hardware—D-rings, wood screws, and wire. The wall hook is rated for 50 pounds.

2 years since mounting

The staghorn has passed plant puberty—the fuzzy brown patch on the undersides of the fingerlike fronds represents spores!

2 years, 4 months

Even with its limited space, the staghorn is starting to push out some babies. Knowing how large they can get, I decided it would be wise to remount the plant with a larger mound of sphagnum moss.

Remounting: The staghorn fern's roots had penetrated the wood, even though I had sealed it with a varnish. I won't bother with the varnish this time.

For this mounting, I created a bedding of sphagnum moss wrapped in burlap, fastened with staples.

I used twine to hold the plant up against the new moss bedding. There's really no way to mount a staghorn fern without damaging the existing shield frond, so don't bother trying to be careful. Just have faith that the next shield

frond will grow over the mounting strings. Look at these babies—now there will be plenty of moss for them to take root!

Bringing the newly mounted trophy back to its growing space.

2 years, 8 months

Remember the three baby staghorns that were growing out from the side? They were so close together that only one managed to put out a fertile frond, while the others were buried.

3 years since mounting

The Platycerium has grown some magnificent fronds that are definitely antlerlike, living up to its name.

String of hearts cuttings
rooting in water.

Sometimes, it can be hard to find a particular species of plant, since a nursery's stock is always rotating. Fortunately, the Internet has made it easy to connect with plant lovers, who tend to be generous with cuttings. Sharing cuttings with your plant-friends is one of the joys of plant parenthood, but learning how to root and grow them is a test of your skill and patience—plus there's the added pressure of not wanting to let your friends down! Here I'm going to explain how to root string of hearts (*Ceropegia woodii*), a vine that I wanted badly and finally got via a few cuttings.

Survival strategy

In daily highs of 200 foot-candles, a string of hearts will survive, but over time, the pattern on its leaves will fade and the distance between leaf sets will increase such that the overall plant begins to feel sparse. You can bring the soil to saturation when it becomes completely dry.

Growth strategy

When the string of hearts can see an hour or two of direct sun, with indirect light at 400–800 foot-candles at other times of the day, the vines will grow nicely, showing strong variegation. As you aerate the soil before watering, take care when probing, as the string of hearts forms thick tubers. Give the soil a good soaking each time it becomes completely dry. When you see active growth, you can fertilize with a balanced fertilizer as directed.

Subjective life span

With a string of hearts, you can be forever propagating and sharing with friends, or carefully managing a long chain for many years. You'll enjoy this plant at any length!

Propagating String of Hearts

Day 1

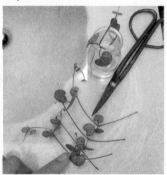  

I prepared these cuttings for rooting by snipping them off just above the node, and they rooted. A more foolproof approach would have been to clip them below the node, removing the leaves that will be submerged in the water. Remember this, because it works for just about any vine-type plant: pothos, philodendron, monstera, ivy, and so forth. Don't be scared—just try it!

Stick the cuttings in water, and make sure the container isn't in direct sun. When each cutting has developed white root tissue, you can transplant. You probably won't have to wait more than four weeks. Leaving the rooted cuttings in water allows you to procrastinate . . . or, rather, wait until you have some time to transplant them.

Use the smallest plastic nursery pot with drainage holes that you have and any light, well-draining soil. I used peat with perlite. Fill the pot with the potting mix and gently tamp it down so it holds the cuttings in place until they take root. I like to group the stems into bundles and space them evenly, using a chopstick as a dibber— that's just a pointed stick to make holes with. The cuttings should stay put because you left the root side as long as possible.

2 months in soil

The plant got to enjoy bright indirect light beside an east-facing window. I measured 300 foot-candles at the brightest point of the day. In terms of watering, this is an "allow soil the dry out between waterings" type of plant.

Why not just bunch them all together and stick that in the soil? That would be too crowded. Why not stick them in individually? Nobody has time for that! Once you have the cuttings in place, water the soil thoroughly but gently—this is where a soft-rain attachment on your watering can is an asset.

3 months in soil

At this point, I could probably
repeat the propagation process if
I wanted a fuller plant, but to me
the appeal of string of hearts
is the dangling vines, and
the plant is doing great!

ZZ Plant

The ZZ plant (*Zamioculcas zamiifolia*) is a low-light succulent that tolerates a great range of light levels and soil
compactness. It's fascinating to watch the growth progression from the "bud" to a full-fledged frond. Basically,
the ZZ plant is a slow grower—you may get just two or
three of these buds each year. When buying a ZZ plant,
I'd recommend looking for a specimen that has a few
unopened stems, so you'll have something fun to witness
over the next few months.

Survival strategy

The ZZ plant is another favorite candi-
date for "thrives in low light." However,
at anything less than 50 foot-candles,
you can expect your ZZ plant to behave
like a green statue. Since the bulbous

OPPOSITE: These photographs of a
growing stem span three months with the
plant in a bright position: Daytime highs
average 400 foot-candles and even some
direct sun for about an hour as it peeks
between the buildings.

ZZ Plant

ABOVE: The ZZ plant's stems do not branch, so you won't be pruning for the purpose of encouraging branching.

RIGHT: As the plant grows, you will encounter a few yellowed stems. Cut these off once they are completely yellow.

base of the stem can store a large amount of water, the soil can be left completely dry for months. Within a few weeks, though, expect to cut off some of the smaller stems as the leaves yellow. You might experience fewer yellowed stems if you aerate the soil occasionally—at this light level, you'll be aerating more often than watering! At the odd times you do water, if you bring the soil to saturation, it would be wise to move the plant right up to a window for a few days so that that water can be utilized. Perhaps you'll "see the light" and leave the plant by that window so it can truly thrive!

Growth strategy

A ZZ plant will grow just fine anywhere from 100 to 1,000 foot-candles. The greater the light intensity, the sooner the soil will become bone dry, which is the right time to water. Since the ZZ plant is tolerant of compacted soil, you can loosen it carefully every other watering. Avoid poking around too close to the stems, because you might pierce the thick underground rhizomes. When you see several new stems emerging, you can safely help them along by fertilizing at this time.

Subjective life span

In lower light, the ZZ plant can act like a green statue, hardly growing but with very little decay. With brighter light, you'll enjoy new stems as older ones flop over. Some may turn yellow or brown—just cut them off. Healthy tubers will keep producing new shoots. Refreshing the soil every few years will help keep things going.

Observations from ZZ Plant Parenthood

Day 1

I chose this ZZ plant because it had two new stems ready to put on a show for the next few months. I thought the rocks would be a nice touch, but I didn't continue with that after the subsequent repottings.

2 months

Roots coming out of drainage holes is the first sign that you should consider checking the root situation inside the pot . . .

. . . and roots coiled up around the bottom of the pot, completely filling the space instead of soil—that's the clear signal to proceed with repotting!

6 months

I was eager to increase my collection of ZZ plants, so I responded to a classified ad for two "established" ZZ plants. Upon closer inspection, the soil looked like outdoor topsoil, which is much too dense and water retaining for the ZZ plant. I unpotted the stems and found they were not even rooted!

Perhaps these could be saved by attempting to root them in water in a corner of my bathroom under a skylight.

10 months

Success! After four months of rooting in water, most of the stems began growing their own rhizomes. They can be transplanted at this point. I added them to my existing ZZ plant, transplanting them into a new, larger pot.

1 year, 4 months

The new amalgamated ZZ plant looks happy—it's putting up new shoots while getting 100 to 200 foot-candles in my bathroom. At this light level, I'm watering roughly on a monthly basis, but I honestly don't keep track.

2 years, 4 months

Many of the older stems are getting floppy, so I've affixed them to a bamboo stake. It's probably ready for another repotting now.

Acknowledgments

Many thanks to all those who opened up their homes for me to photograph and talk about plants:

Jeannie Phan
  @studioplants
Jesse Gold
  @teenytinyterra
Summer Rayne Oakes
  @homesteadbrooklyn
Justine Jeannin
  @sweetyoxalis,
  @whattheflower_paris
Jacqueline Zhou
  @houseplantgal
Melissa Lo
  @melissamlo
Nikhil Tumne
Joseph R. Goldfarb & Alisa G.
  Davis
  @joe.t.o, @whut.club
Claire Kurtin
  @cla1revoyant
Jacqueline Chan
Nancy & Edwin Chan
Carina Chan
Elspeth & Blake Gibson
Violet Sae & Eric Fahn
Susan & Wing Kee
Ashley & Andrew Cheng
Angela & Eric Lee
Orissa Leung
Yoyo Yick

Thank you to the businesses and organizations who welcomed me to photograph their spaces:

Accedo (Toronto office)
  @accedotv
Dynasty
  @dynastytoronto
Northside Espresso + Kitchen
  @northsideespresso
St. Christopher's Anglican Church
  @stchrisanglicanchurch
The Sill
  @thesill
Valleyview Gardens
  @valleyviewgardens

While I've bought my fair share of plants, several sellers have also given me some to try. Thank you for the plants in this book:

Valleyview Gardens
  @valleyviewgardens
Dynasty Toronto
  @dynastytoronto
Crown Flora Studio
  @crownflora
Urban Gardener TO
  @urbangardenerto
Sheridan Nurseries
  @sheridannurseries
Costa Farms
  @costafarms
Filtrum Miami
  @filtrum.miami
The Sill
  @thesill

As the house-plant hobby grows, so, too, will the market for products that are beautifully designed, innovative, and delightful to use. Thanks for the lovely products:

Haws Watering Cans
  @hawswateringcans
Things by HC, Hilton Carter
  @hiltoncarter
The Sill
  @thesill
Homebody Collective
  @homebody.collective
Modernica
  @modernica
Concept Modern
  @eames_addicted

Forage & Lace
  @forageandlace
Beautifully Tarnished
  @beautifully_tarnished
Gardener's Supply Company
  @gardeners
Lee Valley
  @leevalleytools
HPJ Watering Can & Soil Aerator
  @houseplantjournal

Special thanks:

Soumeya B. Roberts:
Thank you for reaching out to me and being the first to see my potential as an author. Your guidance through the whole process has been superb and truly appreciated!

Eric Himmel:
On top of your amazing editing, your ongoing encouragement has helped me through all the ups and downs of the writing process. Thank you, and the team at Abrams—Shawna Mullen, Lisa Silverman, Danielle Youngsmith, and Katie Gaffney—for everything!

Jeannie Phan:
It was a pleasure to work with you, my fellow house-plant blogger. Your illustrations made the key concepts come to life!

Sebit Min:
You made the words and images come together beautifully. Thanks for your amazing work!

Larry Varlese & the Valleyview Gardens team:
You have been a supporter of House Plant Journal from the start. Thanks for showing me around the greenhouses and providing me with many plants.

Eliza Blank & the Sill team:
We had such a wonderful time with you at the shop. Thanks for letting us be part of the team for a few days. My big break on Instagram definitely came from you featuring me all those years ago.

Ricardo Sabino:
Thank you for developing the light meter app with me. I know many will feel a stronger connection to their plants thanks to all your hard work.

Mom (Violet Sae) & Eric Fahn:
Thank you for providing the home where @houseplantjournal started; thank you for your love, support, and tolerance of my indoor jungle! Mom, thank you for all those times you listened to me ramble about the ideas in this book and for teaching me all about outdoor gardening.

Jacqueline Chan:
You have probably heard everything in this book several times over. Thank you for being there through it all—I couldn't have done it without your love and encouragement. Love you lots, my dear!

—Darryl Cheng

Index

Illustrations: Jeannie Phan

Editor: Eric Himmel
Designer: Sebit Min
Production Manager: Kathleen Gaffney

Library of Congress Control Number: 2017956853

ISBN: 978-1-4197-3239-3
eISBN: 978-1-68335-324-9

Abrams Image books are available at special discounts when purchased in quantity for premiums and promotions as well as fundraising or educational use. Special editions can also be created to specification. For details, contact specialsales@abramsbooks.com or the address below.

Abrams Image® is a registered trademark of Harry N. Abrams, Inc.

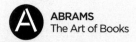

ABRAMS
The Art of Books

195 Broadway
New York, NY 10007
abramsbooks.com